Onward to the Dawn

Onward to the Dawn
A History of Tiffin University

Michael Anthony Grandillo

Tiffin University
155 Miami Street
Tiffin, OH 44883-2161

Reedy Press
PO Box 5131
St. Louis, MO 63139, USA
www.reedypress.com

Library of Congress Control Number: 2010938196
ISBN: 978-1-933370-99-6

Please visit our website at www.reedypress.com.

Cover photograph by Lisa Williams
Photo reproduction and photography by Rob Ledwedge
Design by Jill Halpin

Printed in the United States of America
10 11 12 13 14   5 4 3 2 1

To the memory of my father
Anthony Dominic Grandillo
A true academic

And in honor of

My mother
Lucy DeLuca Grandillo

My loving wife
Nancy Darmour Grandillo

My loving children
Vincent Michael and Gina Rose

And with grateful admiration of and appreciation for my advisor
Dr. Richard C. Perry

Table of Contents

Acknowledgments

Many people and institutions contributed to the completion of this book. I am deeply indebted to a number of people for their support and assistance.

I would like to thank Dr. DeBow Freed, Dr. David Saffell, and William Robinson of Ohio Northern, who were instrumental in helping me begin my career in higher education. I wish to acknowledge the educators of three exceptional institutions of Dayton, Ohio: St. Rita Grade School, Meadowdale High School, and the University of Dayton; together they contributed to my educational foundation for this book.

I received excellent help from librarians. I would like to thank the staff at the Beeghy Library of Heidelberg University and the Pfeiffer Library of Tiffin University. I owe a special debt of gratitude to a meticulous and accomplished young librarian and researcher, Haley Kuhn. Her work in collecting and preserving primary sources and artifacts for this project was immensely valuable.

The writing of this book would not have been possible without the thoughtful criticism and support of a myriad of friends and colleagues, many of whom read the manuscript and provided insight. I would like to thank Charles Ardner; David Boyd; Dr. Charles Christensen; Fran Fleet; Dr. John Millar, Robert Watson, and James White of Tiffin University; Dr. John Bing; Dr. Gary Dickerson, Dr. William Reyer, and Dr. Robert and Dorothy Berg of Heidelberg for their concern and support. Dr. Larry Christman, Dr. Edward Hyland, Beth and Martin Koop, Ericka Kurtz, Dr. John Oliver Jr., Barry Porter, Marilyn Seislove, and Craig Zimmers provided special assistance and support. I will always owe a debt of gratitude to my colleagues in the Office of Development and Public Affairs at Tiffin University. I would like to thank Lori Bentz, Sandy Koehler, Tyson Pinion, and Celinda Scherger. Moreover, to all my friends who said, "When are you ever going to get that thing done?" I thank you.

I wish to add a special word of thanks to President Emeritus George Kidd Jr. and President Paul Marion of Tiffin University, both of whom patiently allowed me to pursue a degree and write this book while in their employ. I am deeply grateful for their personal support and financial assistance.

This book began as a dissertation, and few PhD candidates have been as well served as I. I would like to thank Dr. David Meabon, the late Dr. Charles Glaab, and my advisor and chair, Dr. Richard C. Perry of the University of Toledo. Without Dr. Perry's support, this book would not have been possible.

Finally, my largest debts are to my family: to my children, Vincent and Gina, and above all, my wife, Nancy. Thank you for your sacrifices and loving support.

Foreword

In the late 1800s and early 1900s men and women eager to benefit from an expanding American industrial and commercial economy sought empowerment through education. Tiffin University's success in these years illustrates how a new class of educational entrepreneurs met these expectations in dramatically new ways. Dr. Grandillo offers the reader a concrete example of the controversies, challenges, and successes of business education from the early years of the twentieth century to the first decade of the twenty-first. Often reading like a suspenseful adventure narrative, the story of this bold, brash, upstart experiment in higher education offers a compelling account of entrepreneurship and innovation in American life.

Tiffin University's struggle to achieve recognition and acceptance for its innovative approach to commercial education mirrored a larger social conflict pitting a new generation of educators against the nineteenth-century traditions of post-secondary education. Dr. Grandillo's analysis of the rise of Tiffin University from its beginnings as a largely independent part of Heidelberg University in the nineteenth century to an economically viable, nationally recognized leader in business education by the 1930s gives concrete form to the intellectual, social, and institutional battles of the period. Tiffin University's subsequent new beginning in the last decades of the twentieth century, merging practical instruction with elements of a traditional education, brings the school's history full circle.

The story begins in the late nineteenth century when the Commercial Department of Heidelberg University was a less-than-favored stepchild of the overall university. After a period of struggle, they mutually agreed to separate, and then followed very different paths. During the first decades of the twentieth century, the two Millers—Heidelberg University's president Charles E. Miller and Tiffin Business University's president F. J. Miller—were noted antagonists. One spoke for the traditional "classical" education of Greek and Latin, philosophy and religion; the other for concrete commercial skills that would empower young men and women seeking well-paid employment. One emphasized the overriding worth of established truths and traditional sources of knowledge, while the other advocated practical abilities. One derided a developing emphasis on money and consumption; the other welcomed a "success" culture that offered commercial workers and business employees a middle-class lifestyle. One defended the privilege and cultural attainments of an old established order; the other offered upward mobility to an expanding population of young men and women suspicious of abstract thought and committed to developing employable skills. While both schools found relative success in their separate missions, Dr. Grandillo focuses on the remarkable rise of Tiffin University, illustrating the changing nature of higher education in the state of Ohio during the first half of the twentieth century.

Dr. Grandillo's narrative of the success of Tiffin University brings the saga of the struggle between traditional and practical education into the twenty-first century, as he chronicles the current extent to which the two traditions are being reintegrated in today's multipurpose university. For as Heidelberg University has broadened its curriculum to include professional programs, Tiffin University has become a diverse and comprehensive university, embracing the "liberal arts" tradition as well as practical courses and programs of study.

Dr. Grandillo writes with obvious approval of these efforts, praising the work of President Williard of Heidelberg in the 1880s and Drs. Kidd and Marion in the 1990s and 2000s to resolve such conflicts and to accommodate and treat fairly different programs and objectives within a university framework. Presently, he believes, we see in the success of Tiffin University how inspired leadership can successfully integrate classical learning, scientific knowledge, and practical skills within a single institution. Today two men of imagination and vision lead Tiffin University and Heidelberg University as both schools attempt to affirm not just the compatibility but the necessary unity of these two goals of higher education. Since "the jury is still out" on the success of such efforts, Dr. Grandillo's account of the battle between these two approaches to higher education in early twentieth-century Tiffin is not only an enjoyable chronicle of larger-than-life personalities and the development of Tiffin University, but also an important and instructive narrative for our own time.

John Bing
Professor of Political Science and Anthropology
Heidelberg University

Introduction

Onward to the Dawn is the first history of Tiffin University, an institution more than 120 years old. From its founding as a for-profit commercial college at Heidelberg College to its slow but dramatic transformation into a successful independent university, the history of Tiffin University is a series of exceptional events that add to the historiography of higher education.

Almost every city and village in America in the late nineteenth century had a small commercial college teaching bookkeeping and business-related skills. Few of these enterprises survived; even fewer transitioned and transformed into a modern university. Tiffin University is a story of endurance and struggle, commitment and challenge, transition and transformation. It is a story that needs to be told.

No comprehensive analysis places the university in a historical context, especially in view of its impact on higher education and the state of Ohio. The available literature on the history of Tiffin University is limited. The small number of internal documents produced were never widely disseminated prior to 1981. A university publication, *The Challenge Magazine,* has been published since then to inform alumni and friends. It has served as the document of record ever since. It has published, at times, articles of a his-

toric nature. An article of special note, written for the occasion of the university's centennial in 1988, was *TU: Our Beginnings*, written by historian and Heidelberg College archivist Carl G. Klopfenstein.[1] It is an outstanding account of the founding and early years (1888–1917) and chronicles the time Tiffin University, titled the Commercial College at that time, was associated with Heidelberg College. It supports the fact that the Commercial College during that time was always a separate institution within the framework of Heidelberg College and that the Commercial College was founded in 1888.

Until recently, almost all state surveys of collegiate institutions and higher education histories omitted Tiffin University. The absence of chronicling the history of Tiffin University presents a gap in higher education institutional knowledge, as well as local historical knowledge. The exception occurred in 2003, with *Cradles of Conscience: Ohio's Independent Colleges and Universities,*[2] edited by James A. Hodges, James H. O'Donnell, and John William Oliver Jr. In honor of the state of Ohio's bicentennial, a group of scholars, led by historian John William Oliver of Malone College, sought to compile a collection of histories on the independent colleges of Ohio emphasizing the institutions' early years, the mission of their founders, and how the institutions changed over time. At first, as in the past, Tiffin University was not originally slated for inclusion. Professor Oliver recognized the oversight and a last-minute call to this author resulted in an eighteen-page interpretive essay on the history of Tiffin University. It is the only one ever published.

This book began as a dissertation, and it now stands as a new historical analysis of the creation and evolution of Tiffin University, focusing on its first fifty years. In the historiography of education, this work falls neatly into the institutional history genre. A hybrid use of qualitative and quantitative research techniques were used in this book. More than five thousand written documents, statistical sources, oral interviews, artifacts, and relics were subject to critical review and evaluation, resulting in a historical narrative. John R. Thelin's model to create distinctive, connecting, and contributing college institutional histories was used. He suggests a writer should strive to create horizontal histories, in contrast to vertical histories. Horizontal histories connect distinctive attributes, subcultures, and trends to broader historical issues.[3] They better trace the development of academic programs and link campus events to other social, political, and economic movements of the day and result in a more lively and thicker narrative.

Most importantly, institutions are groups of people; this history tells the story of the individuals who, by their sheer determination and vision, built a modern university. Naturally, humans can experience both conflict and cooperation. The artful leadership and risk taking of a few individuals changed Tiffin University. Responding to severe periods of instability or societal change, the leadership of the university seized critical moments in history to strengthen and unify its culture and, in turn, mastered educational delivery. This research illuminates how individual actions shape history. Tiffin University achieved and prospered when it acted as a community of people and was led by presidents with transformational leadership qualities espousing a shared vision. The findings also illustrate the power of a common institutional vision.

During its first thirty years, Tiffin University was affiliated with Heidelberg College as a financially independent and separate division or college, known as the Commercial College. It taught business courses typically found in the popular commercial colleges of the day. After breaking with Heidelberg College in 1917, the Commercial College of Heidelberg was moved by Franklin J. Miller and Alfred M. Reichard to a rented second-story building in downtown Tiffin. These men purchased the college from John Sterner in 1909. They successfully operated it in downtown Tiffin as Tiffin Business University from 1917 to 1939.

The for-profit Tiffin Business University became non-profit Tiffin University in 1939. Tiffin University moved to an abandoned public elementary school building in a west-side Tiffin neighborhood in 1956 after thirty-nine years in its downtown Tiffin location. Tiffin University struggled for the next twenty-five years to expand curricula, secure accreditation, and build a physical plant. A milestone occurred when George Kidd Jr. assumed the presidency in 1981. There was talk of closing the school or merging it with another institution when he became president. President Kidd quickly launched the most explosive growth in the institution's history. His twenty-one-year tenure can be characterized as transforming a small, financially troubled business school into a comprehensive, modern university. Paul Marion was named president in 2002 and is now taking the institution to new levels.

The history of Tiffin University tells us how higher education responded to historic periods, trends, and external environments, such as the Industrial Revolution, the Gilded Age, the rise of the middle class, and the development of the state of Ohio. The history of Tiffin University is also the story of the rise of the commercial college and business education in the United States. Despite their early successes, little has been written about the commercial college's historic past or present-day impact. Higher education's response to these and other historic events is both informative and important in understanding American economic and political culture.

One can have a better understanding of the historical roots of the liberal arts curriculum by reaching back far beyond the Italian Renaissance. This helps clarify the role of commercial or practical education in Europe and America. This saga begins, fittingly, amid the conflict of the liberal and practical arts. How this duality evolved in the last five centuries provides an essential backdrop to collegiate education of the twenty-first century. Educational foundations laid in the fifteenth century are responsible for both the American liberal arts curriculum and the practical arts, including business education. A careful review and understanding of this quintessential educational struggle shows that their dialectic debates helped create modern higher education. Tiffin University's genesis, survival, and success come out of these advancements and struggles. Its gains have been the results of artful responses to adversity and opportunity.

End Notes

1   Carl G Klopfenstein, "TU: Our Beginnings," *The Challenge Magazine* (Fall 1988): 17.

2   Michael A. Grandillo, "Tiffin University: Risk and Gain" in *Cradles of Conscience: Ohio Independent Colleges and Universities*, ed. James A. Hodges, James H. O'Donnell, and John W. Oliver (Kent, Ohio: Kent State University Press, 2003), 442–452.

3   Frederick Rudolph and John R. Thelin, *The American College and University: A History* (Athens: University of Georgia Press, 1990).

Onward to the Dawn

Chapter 1

{The United States at the dawn of the nineteenth century, by Daniel Ligars, 1806. Birmingham Public Library Cartography Collection. Courtesy of the University of Alabama Map Library, Craig Remington.}

The United States
and Higher Education

The formation of fields of study into an educational philosophy—the liberal arts education in particular—developed over centuries. Rome formatted its version of the essential fields of study from the Greeks, and in turn, Roman educational thought was adapted by Christian ideals and passed on through the Middle Ages. The educational aims of liberal arts were Greek in origin and survived for 1,500 years of adaptation that defined Renaissance educational thought and still impact education today. The struggle between the *useful* and *practical arts* and *liberal arts* has always been debated. As the liberal arts were formalized and condensed, the practical arts were separated from what would develop the mind, thus creating a division of fields of study. This centuries-old debate was formed and shaped by social, political, and economic forces throughout time.[1]

The Civil War's Impact on Higher Education

From the founding of Harvard College in 1636 until 1800, only eighteen colleges served just four hundred students in the United States. Although the number of colleges grew exponentially in the nineteenth century, the educational philosophy of higher education in the United States remained consistent until after the Civil War. Colleges founded before the Civil War are known as classical colleges, or literary or oldtime colleges.[2] Classical colleges reflect the following characteristics: small in nature, religious, regionally parochial, and deeply fixed on a classical curriculum dominated by Latin and Greek. Expanding beyond the classical curriculum was outside the purposes of their founding.

As the demand for science and technical education became more prevalent, the usefulness of a curriculum dedicated to the training of clergy and gentlemen was questioned. This debate raged in the early nineteenth century and culminated with the Yale Report of 1826. Jeremiah Day, the president of Yale College, wrote the report in response to his trustees' concerns on the efficacy of a classical education. His argument for a general classical curriculum was grounded in the notion that colleges should not teach something that is peculiar to a specific profession or trade.[3]

The classical college, embracing the essence of the Yale Report, did not change much from the founding of Harvard until the Civil War. These colleges were vigorous in their instruction and socially rigid, with some variations. They considered their approach educationally superior and disparaged other forms of education, especially those that responded to societal needs and market demands.[4] The classical college of the nineteenth century never appealed to a large segment of the population, and their enrollments reflected this. Toward the end of the century, classical colleges would have no choice but to adapt themselves to a new perception of the utility of higher education in the United States.

The period between 1860 and 1880 brought many significant changes in higher education that set the foundation for a broader scope of university organization and forced classical colleges to recognize a number of new disciplines of specialized education. The passage of the Morrill Act of 1862, which began the utilitarian land grant movement; the advent of the elective system by Charles Elliot of Harvard; the increasing acceptance of technical education; the favorable reception of coeducation; and the founding of colleges dedicated to African Americans are important examples of innovations in this period. Institutions of higher education became more democratic and egalitarian. In the 1890s the chapter-owned house became a reality and gave a physical presence to the fraternity movement.[5] By branching out to rising educational markets, colleges were more in concert with the American democratic ideal of opportunity. A greater acceptance and readiness to add new and different fields of study allowed teacher education, the

sciences, technical training, and short courses in commercial subjects into the college ranks.[6]

As urban centers sprang up across the nation in the late nineteenth century, classical colleges, still fervently adhering to a rigid curriculum, began to see increasing competition for students from emerging institutions, which focused on societal needs. No real job or profession in post–Civil War America required the classical college's bachelor's degree for employment.[7] In contrast, challenging the existing order, normal schools trained teachers; medical schools prepared doctors, dentists, and pharmacists; and commercial colleges developed shop clerks and accountants. Educational institutions were now shaped by the cultural and business contexts in the communities they served.

The Civil War also brought profound changes in the way individuals viewed American higher education. Many Civil War veterans and others sought a vocational education. Many felt the Civil War was won not only on the battlefield but also on the railroad and in the factory. A long call for more business, science, and engineering education began in the 1860s and 1870s, resulting in the reforms of the 1880s. Confederate General Robert E. Lee endorsed this movement in his postwar role as president of Washington College, adding commercial education as well as engineering and modern languages to the classical curriculum of the college, which would later add his name.[8] New institutions increased educational opportunities in a variety of capacities.[9]

The stage was set for an educational transformation from the sleepy classical college of antebellum America to the multipurpose university of the twentieth century. This transformation saw rapid acceleration in the last decades of the nineteenth century.[10]

The German model of the secular, modern, research-based university emerged in the two decades following the Civil War. By 1870, more than ten thousand Americans had studied abroad in German universities.[11] They returned deeply impressed with the scientifically based and professionally organized German university model. The experiences of this internationally educated professorate inspired a change in American higher education. The influx of German-educated Americans promoted the adoption of German standards for scholarship and university structure. Innovations such as increased delineation between preparatory and higher learning, increased academic independence for students and teachers, the introduction of the Doctor of Philosophy degree—the Ph.D.—as a standard for quantifying research ability, and the importance of advancing knowledge and training through research provided a framework for a new academic structure. The German university system, with some modifications, was accepted in the New World and began to take root. Although graduate education gained in importance in the United States, the German model of independent graduate schools outside existing institutions did not develop in America. When graduate education was added, it remained directly associated with the university.[12]

The graduate schools at Johns Hopkins University, the University of Chicago, Cornell University, and the University of Michigan became the university standard in modern America. Concurrently, modern academic disciplines such as history, economics, chemistry, and others developed and were accepted into the American college and university curricula. Academic departments became the standard construct for institutional organization. As a result, departments of like-minded academics developed. These emerging ideas and key innovations permeated all higher education in the late nineteenth century. Academic innovation was not limited to the new research-oriented universities. Most existing colleges, formed as classical colleges, were forced by these cultural and societal pressures to change and incorporate many of the innovations promulgated during this time.

Higher Education in The Gilded Age

After the Civil War, America experienced rapid industrialization in the North while renewing western expansion, which sustained the overall growth rate of the nation. The South, slow to recover from the war, reconstruction, and a lackluster growth in the cotton trade, entered into a period of regional decline.

Clearly, the rapid growth of the railroad system was an important factor in the economic development of the United States from the Civil War to the turn of the century. A national transportation network, technological changes, economies of scale, and mass production added fuel to the industrial revolution and

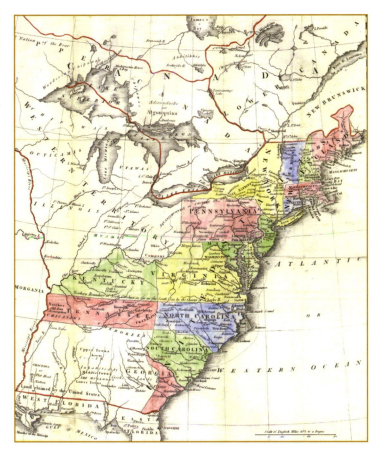

{The United States and its Western Territory, circa 1803. Courtesy Larry Christman.}

became the main engines of the economy. During this time, the American economy took on many of its enduring characteristics; chiefly, the impressive change from an agricultural society to an industrial one. Although this shift was developing for some time, the 1890 census[13] reported for the first time that manufacturing outpaced agriculture in dollar-value output. By the mid-1890s, America had become the world's leading industrial power, outpacing Europe, including Germany and the United Kingdom. This growth created new jobs—many of which needed commercial college training. The 1880s became a period of rapid change in both commerce and higher education.[14]

In the 1880s, higher education realized what it has known since the Renaissance, that no institution is ever fully developed and complete and is never independent of market forces, societal changes, and forces generated within itself. Thus, higher education in the 1880s changed in response to the times. New fields became a legitimate part of study.[15] Early normal schools quickly developed to provide needed teachers for the multiplying elementary schools. The expansion of business training paralleled the expansion of America's industrial and economic life, which characterized this period. Many institutions began to boldly say that a direct vocational objective was acceptable and had always revealed itself in new or existing academic programs influenced by societal and economic conditions.

Development of Business Education in America

Business education in America endured three distinct transformations: the rudimentary apprentice system; the proprietary commercial college; and the modern, university-affiliated business college. Business education was called commercial education from the early nineteenth century until well into the twentieth century.[16] Understanding the three stages of business education evolution allows us to see how business education in America developed and the historical context in which Tiffin University evolved.

The apprentice system was a common way to train young men in business from the Colonial times until the mid-nineteenth century.[17] Business education's development from apprenticeship to proprietary institution to university setting mirrors that of other professions such as law and medicine. The student associated himself as an employee for an established mercantile and served in a student relationship, with the owner/operator imparting to him the ways of the business and commerce. The mentor/student or master/apprenticeship relationship provided the student with personal attention and instruction in a variety of business techniques and social and political skills while acquiring shared community values. The apprentice worked alongside the owner and, at times, even lived in the owner's house. With markets local and production simple, a successful transfer of knowledge took place. As markets widened and demands for goods increased, the need for more trained workers exceeded the number that could be trained in this one-on-one manner.

During this time, academies and evening schools were established in larger cities to supplement the education an apprentice needed. The evolution of business education was also augmented by the introduction of textbooks promoting the Italian method of bookkeeping and other business techniques. The earliest business text used in the colonies appeared in 1736. *Bookkeeping Methodized: A Methodical Treatise on Merchant Accounts According to the Italian Form,* by John Mair[18] was popular in the mid-eighteenth century and was reprinted several times. Its sixth edition was published in 1760. This work, and others such as Thomas Dilworth's *The Young Bookkeeper's Assistant,*[19] Benjamin Workman's *American Accountant,*[20] and James Maginness' *The Student's Assistant, Containing a Concise Method of Bookkeeping,* are noted for their early instructional value.[21] Thus they served as textbooks in early schools, as well as a foundation for the proprietor/teacher role, which is the basis of the early commercial college.

The private business school, normally called a commercial college, was the second intermediate stage of business education development in the United States. A quintessential American institution, the commercial college dominated business education in America from the mid-nineteenth century until well into the twentieth century.[22] They have been one of the major purveyors of business education in America since first appearing in the early nineteenth century. These colleges filled a burgeoning need for trained business workers and were strictly business ventures. Commercial colleges were proprietary in nature. Commercial colleges typically taught bookkeeping, ornamental penmanship, modest business practices, and later typewriting and shorthand. The owners were very good marketers, which challenged the existing educational establishment. This right of ownership in an educational institution is in concert with the nineteenth-century professional schools, including medicine and law. However, it is in contrast with the classical colleges of the time, which were strictly eleemosynary institutions.

Higher education scholarship in the 1920s sought to qualify the periods of growth in the commercial college movement and to bring some understanding of the wave of business education development prevalent in the 1920s. The commercial college in the United States experienced three phases of development, according to Cloyd Marvin.[23] The first was the experimental (1834–1850), when the first schools were organized and the curriculum was standardized. The second phase was the monopolistic period (1850–1890), when commercial colleges dominated the field of business education and became fierce competition for classical collegiate education. The final phase was the modern period (1890 to the present), where business education expanded to all education venues, and commercial colleges had to compete with both secondary schools and universities. Charles Reigner[24] also added delineation to the commercial college movement by providing historical periods. He divided the eras of development into the period of individual initiative (1820–1853); the period of concerted action (1853–1866); and the period of expansion (1866–1890). Marvin and Reigner both contend that the private commercial college dominated the business education landscape until about 1890, when they gave way to sharing the business education market with high schools and universities.

The third stage of business development in America was when institutions of collegiate rank incorporated business education into its curriculum. As a response to the popularity of business education in commercial colleges and the unsatisfied need for educated business leadership created by America's commercial prowess, higher education formally welcomed business education into its curriculum in the 1880s. The collegiate school of business was a final response to a need for formal university business education. The period between 1900 and 1925 was a time when colleges, schools, departments, and courses of business administration were added to the university curriculum at fever pitch. Cubberley, in *The History of Education*, provides a 1920 perspective on the educational movement that transitioned from the commercial college to the university:

The industrial life of the nation has become more diversified, its parts narrower, and its processes more concealed, new and more extended training has been called for to prepare young people to meet the intricacies and interdependence of political and industrial and social groups and to point out to them the importance of each one's part in the national and industrial organization.[25]

Founded in 1881, the Wharton School of Finance and Economy at the University of Pennsylvania was the first known separate division dedicated to business education to be directly affiliated with a university. A $100,000 gift by Joseph Wharton, a Philadelphia merchant and manufacturer, made possible the addition of the new school.[26]

The Wharton School stood alone for seventeen years until the University of Chicago founded the College of Commerce and Politics and the University of California added its College of Commerce in

Table 1.

Early Business Programs in Ohio

Year	College or University	Type of Business Education Program
1909	Ohio University	School of Commerce
1911	St. Xavier College	Department of Commerce and Economics
1915	Ohio State University	College of Commerce
1916	University of the City of Toledo	Department of Commerce
1916	Defiance College	Course in Economics and Business Administration
1918	Muskingum College	Department of Economics and Business Administration
1920	Ohio Wesleyan University	Department of Economics and Business Administration
1921	Mt. Union College	Course in Economics and Business Administration
1921	University of Dayton	College of Commerce and Finance
1921	Antioch College	Department of Industrial Management and Business
1922	Western Reserve University	Major in Business Administration
1923	Wittenberg College	Department of Business Administration
1923	Miami University	Division of Business

1898. Dartmouth College, the University of Vermont, the University of Wisconsin, and New York University added divisions of business education, bringing the total to seven at the dawn of the new century.[27] The next twenty-five years saw brisk acceptance of business education at the collegiate level, and the period between 1915 and 1925 saw the most explosive growth. By 1925, more than 183 American colleges and universities, including thirteen in Ohio, had officially added an organized academic structure dedicated to business.[28]

The Commercial College in America

Institutions providing instruction in business and commerce in the United States developed rapidly between the Civil War and World War I. The transition of the American economy from local family businesses to global corporations spurred this expansion. Business or commercial education became a movement in the 1880s, arising from the growth of the American economy and the public need that accompanied it. Although early ideals of education and business were dramatically opposed, American businessmen turned to privately owned commercial colleges as a source to train employees.

Table 2.

Enrollment Comparison of Colleges and Universities and Commercial Colleges, 1879–1880 and 1889–1890

	1879–1880		1889–1890	
	Institutions	**Students**	**Institutions**	**Students**
Colleges and Universities	671	50,816	657	65,700
Commercial Colleges	162	27,146	263	78,920

Since no existing academic framework responded to the need of business education, for-profit entrepreneurs took up the call to start commercial schools. They formed in an unsystematic way, responding to the abundance of young men eager to enter the field of business. The moneymaking spirit of the owners of the schools played an important part in the advancement of the commercial college. Quality varied from school to school, and vast sums were spent on advertising—an activity that still receives mixed acceptability today. However, the high competition in commercial colleges from 1880 to 1910 raised the standard of education and eliminated the charlatan nature of some of its owners. Most traditional colleges dismissed the commercial college development even though they served as the foundation for future schools of business. Despite occasional unethical activities and their aggressive advertising, the private commercial school flourished, providing a needed educational service. Commercial education could be found across the educational spectrum, in high schools, in normal schools, and in col-

leges and universities by the 1890s.[29] Following their initial appearance in the 1850s, the number of commercial colleges grew to twenty-six by 1870, with more than 5,800 students enrolled.[30] The institutions varied in quality, and most were modest operations; courses in elementary bookkeeping and ornamental penmanship were quickly augmented by courses in stenography, typewriting, and secretarial training. Graduates of these colleges quickly filled the need of a growing business community for trained individuals.

Commercial colleges played an important role in the lives of the nation's foremost industrialists. Andrew Carnegie, Johns Hopkins, John D. Rockefeller, and others attended commercial colleges in the 1800s. They, in turn, used their fortunes to later change American higher education through their philanthropic boosts.[31]

Commercial colleges' success as profitable ventures speaks to their rapid development between 1870 and 1900. By 1900, more than 400 commercial colleges enrolled more than 110,000 students, including 65,000 men and 45,000 women.[32] Education and business were fused, clearly recognizing the utility of their mutual interests.

History of Accounting Education

Although evidence of records and accounting practices dates back to Biblical times,[33] accounting practices and education used today trace their origin to medieval Italy. Double-entry bookkeeping, a stable focus of early American commercial colleges, was developed in late thirteenth- or early fourteenth-century Italy. Double-entry bookkeeping saw widespread application in Renaissance Italy far before Fra Luca Pacioli published the first manual in 1494.[34] No accounting innovation matched the Italian method of double entry for the next three hundred years. Italian and later Dutch merchants slowly introduced double-entry debits and credits throughout Europe and England. An English translation of Pacioli in 1543 and ensuing works made this business advancement available for wider distribution in England by 1600. Employment of double-entry bookkeeping made significant contributions to the economic growth of England, and by the late eighteenth century it was heavily used in business activities.[35]

As the colonists introduced a number of business customs to the New World, demand for bookkeeping grew with the advancement of the colonies. The training and education of business practices, including accounting, was confined to apprenticeship and learning from others. Few books existed. The first book on ac-counting published in America was William Mitchell's *A New and Complete System of Bookkeeping* in 1796.[36] One of the first records of teaching bookkeeping in the new United States of America was in Portland, Maine. Thomas Turner instructed students either personally or in small groups if they purchased his early book on accounting: *An Epitome of Bookkeeping by Double Entry.*[37] Teaching bookkeeping served as the foundation of commercial education. James Bennett, one of the earliest American writers on bookkeeping, published *The American System of Practical Bookkeeping.*[38] His popularity with educators and practitioners led him to start a school in New York in 1814, dedicated to training bookkeepers.

History of Penmanship Science

The workings of commerce—the interchange of goods and commodities—required a tremendous amount of written material. Penmanship, or hand-writing, was one of the essential branches of learning taught in commercial colleges well into the 1930s. No student could hope to obtain a position in commerce without the mastery of penmanship.

Penmanship in Colonial America was considered a necessary business skill. Daybooks, ledgers, receipts, bills of lading, waste books, invoices, and all forms of business correspondence entailed the art of penmanship.[39] The teaching of penmanship and its importance to mercantile ventures, popular in England and throughout Europe since the mid-seventeenth century, made its way to the New World. Business academies were first formed in London to teach business in the early 1800s, and they placed penmanship at the foundation of the curriculum. Thomas Watts, who ran one of the first private business academies in London, gave penmanship primacy in his small school. In his treatise, *An Essay on the Proper Method for Forming the Man of Business,* Watts stated:

Whoever will be a Man of Business, must be a Man of Correspondence . . . and, correspondence can never be so commodiously or at all to the Purpose maintained or by the use of the Pen: So that writing is the First Step, and Essential in Business.[40]

Watts, who set the standard in business education for almost a century, promoted and taught the education skills a businessman needed for success. He ranked penmanship as first in importance, followed by arithmetic and accounting. Penmanship, arithmetic, and accounting slowly became the staples of mercantile business skills in Europe and America. Newly formed academies and business schools soon filled the demand for learning these skills.

Handwriting was a male-dominated profession and took on an apprentice-type method of instruction. Circuit teachers found themselves in high demand, providing private lessons and forming temporary new schools. Centered in Eastern port cities, advertisements and broadsides promoting penmanship classes abounded. Penmanship was widely accepted in eighteenth-century America as a foundation of business. The commercial colleges that later emerged in almost every city in America by the late nineteenth century featured penmanship. Penmanship was taught in private academies and later in public and private schools. Handwriting books, often called copybooks,[41] were used to teach handwriting and served as a reinforcement of the link between penmanship and commerce using business forms and business sayings as examples to copy. By the mid-eighteenth century, writing masters operated private academies that offered a full business curriculum. Their texts were penned by the writing masters of the day. Thus, instruction in penmanship overlapped with arithmetic, accounting, and other subjects. Manuals, such as George Fisher's *The American Instructor: Or Young Man's Best Companion,* provided students with both a self-tutoring manual and a triumvirate of commercial business skills.[42]

Before the 1850s, writing instructors, beyond selling copybooks and teaching proper writing techniques, provided important instruction in the creation and selection of writing instruments. Steel pens did not widely replace quills until the mid-1800s. Before that, the proper selection and cutting of quills was an important part of handwriting instruction. Goose, raven, and crow quills performed differently, and manipulating quills to take ink and deliver it in a fine line on paper required more than proper penmanship. The art of penmanship, and that of the proper cutting of quills, became American tools of business important to the emerging mercantile middle class.

With the advent of the steel pen, first handmade and later factory produced, more people gained access to the art of penmanship. At the same time, copybooks were mass produced and became more available. Penmanship shifted from the manipulation of writing tools to a more complex theory on handwriting positions, which included the breakdown of components of letters such as ovals, curves, and strokes. The demand for this education rose as accelerated capital accumulation helped spur reforms in higher education, simultaneously broadening offerings to include business education.

Platt Roger Spencer was one of the earliest promoters of penmanship theory. He helped transform business education in America. Spencer was the first to advance a new style of penmanship training and education. He is considered the most successful writing master of the Victorian era; so successful, in fact, that his style of handwriting was, and still is, called *Spencerian*.[43] At an early age, he was known for his dominance in penmanship education. Both a perceptive businessman and a philosopher of his day, Spencer created a handwriting empire that embraced public and private penmanship education at every level.

With penmanship at the foundation of his educational enterprises, Spencer became the first to promote business education in such an organized and systematic way that his schools soon multiplied across the country. Starting in Northern Ohio at age fifteen, he organized business colleges and normal schools with an early partner, Victor Rice. The popularity of his handwriting method brought great acclaim to his schools, as he augmented his penmanship courses with bookkeeping and other mercantile skills.

His textbooks were widely sought after and used in all levels of education.

After his death in 1864, Spencer became even more popular due to the clever marketing and business acumen of his relatives and friends, who branched out with entrepreneurial fervor, founding and leading Spencerian Business Colleges throughout the United States. His friends and heirs quickly copyrighted his works and issued a complete set of textbooks in series form. The use of these texts, and their consistency and quality, helped ensure that the replication of Spencerian Business Colleges remained strong educational enterprises. By the late 1890s, Spencerian Business Colleges were in forty-two states and became a model for business education.[44] Other resourceful and entrepreneurial men joined Spencer in founding franchises of commercial colleges across the United States, most notably George Eastman of Rochester, New York, and H. B. Bryant and H. D. Stratton of Buffalo, New York. The Bryant and Stratton franchise grew to more than fifty schools in the late 1800s, and fifteen of the original schools still provide career-oriented education today.

The Impact of the Typewriter

Four hundred years after the advent of moveable type, the next progressive step in communication was invented: the typewriter. The first patent for a typewriter was awarded in London in 1741; however, any significant use of the typewriting machine was not evident until one hundred years later when the Bain and Wright Typing Machine received some acclaim in

London in 1841. The first American typewriting patent was awarded in 1843. The early invention was slowly improved throughout the next forty years.[45]

The Industrial Revolution and its impact on modern methods of conducting business spread the impact of the typewriter and promoted it as a central business tool in all forms of communication. As a storm of commercialism swept late nineteenth-century America, so did the rapid development of the wide distribution and use of the typewriter. The typewriter superseded handwriting in the business world as the central office became prominent in business management. It mechanized routine and dreary office work usually conducted by hand. Training on this new business machine became essential to the success of enterprises. Commercial colleges became the place of choice to learn this new skill. Training evolved in concert with the rapid improvements of the manufacturing of the typewriter in the 1880s. Typewriting education centered on two things: The selection of the best method of education and the mechanical development of the typewriter. Commercial colleges played a role in both of these developments.

The 1870s was the Age of Invention, which buoyed the Industrial Revolution in the United States. In 1874, Christopher Latham Sholes, Carlos Glidden, and Samuel Sholes were the first Americans to invent a typewriter that enjoyed some promise. They developed and patented the Sholes and Glidden Typewriter in the Kleinsteubens Machine Shop in Milwaukee, Wisconsin. It was not a great success. The typewriter failed to surpass the handwritten word, in large part because it was slower than handwriting and could only type capital letters. This quickly changed when they sold their patent and manufacturing rights, later that year, to E. Remington and Sons, the successful gun and sewing machine manufacturers. Remington introduced an improved addition, the Remington No. 2, in 1878. It found immediate acceptance. The Remington No. 2 created the double strike stick and shift, allowing both upper- and lower-case letters to be typed at one time. The timeliness of the invention coincided with the need for educated and trained commercial workers and new efficiencies demanded by industry. Simultaneously, Remington founded a worldwide industry. Commercial education quickly responded by providing the training needed on this new, highly demanded product.[46]

As the typewriter demand increased, so did the methods used to teach the new art. Early commercial college teachers experimented with methods to increase speed and accuracy. Around 1880, Frank McGurrin was the first to develop a touch system that did not require looking at the keys. His method, however, only used three fingers. Separately, Mrs. M. V. Longley, a teacher in a commercial college in Cincinnati, developed a system using all fingers. She published her ideas, with the help of the Remington Company, in an instruction book titled *Remington Typewriting Lessons*. Remington and other companies made typewriters accessible at a reasonable cost to commercial colleges. Demand for training in the touch system of typing increased as the influence of the typewriter permeated industry. Typewriting education grew into a prominent movement at the same time commercial colleges were booming. Typewriting education was commonplace in commercial colleges by 1890.[47]

Local Booster Movement and Higher Education

Daniel Boorstin, author of *The Americans: The Democratic Experience* and *The Americans: The Colonial Experience*,[48] is most emphatic in promoting the importance of the concept of local boosterism in the development of colleges and universities. In *The Americans: The Democratic Experience*, Boorstin states that America was a nation of consumption communities where cities and towns sought economic prizes such as railroads, county seats, hotels, and most importantly, a college. The college, as a nineteenth-century economic development tool, joined these other community institutions in creating community spirit and giving these cities and new towns a competitive advantage. A new college was both a tangible and intangible monument. In *The Americans: The Colonial Experience*, Boorstin argues that American colleges were emphatically institutions of the local communities. No community was complete without a college. He reiterates this concept in *Hidden Histories: Exploring Our Secret Past,* announcing that colleges "are monuments to community . . . they are originated in the community, depend on the community, are developed by the community, serve the community, and

rise and fall with the community."[49] Failure to boost one's city showed a lack of community spirit and a lack of business sense. Colleges and their relationship to a community became an important part of American life. The Dartmouth decision—a landmark Supreme Court ruling in 1819 that secured Dartmouth, and other colleges, as private, rather than public, entities—influenced many aspects of private higher education in the United States, but an often overlooked point has been that the case solidified a private institution's governing boards, deepening the board members' commitment and the college's attachment to the community.

This communitarian booster spirit grew to become a nineteenth-century phenomenon. The growth of cities and towns in America preceded organized governmental political subdivisions. Local boosters created a spirit that solved public needs long before the government did.[50] As the physical features of towns and cities began to grow, so did the spirit of the community. Boorstin states, "This notion of community is one of the most characteristic, one of the most important, yet one of the least noticed American contributions to modern life."[51] All of this proved well for the private, non-governmental college in nineteenth-century Ohio. Thus, this nineteenth-century phenomenon of the individual local booster and the concept of local boosterism became institutionalized in American social culture. These quintessentially American concepts self-actualized in the late nineteenth century when the word *booster* was invented

{The Beaux Arts Seneca County Courthouse was built at the height of the Gilded Age in 1884. The original clock tower, shown here, was replaced with an Art Deco–style tower in the 1940s. At one time, present-day Tiffin University (corner of Miami and Sandusky) was highly considered as a site for the courthouse.}

in 1890, and *boosterism* became etymologically accepted in the early twentieth century.[52]

While some historians argue that the social and cultural struggles after the Civil War expanded the role of colleges and universities, they do not discount the marriage between "the agents of ethnoreligious subcultures and local boosterism," as William Leslie noted in his book, *Gentleman and Scholars: College and Community in the Age of the University—1865–1917*.[53] Competition of all sorts created colleges and universities. This included religious groups, but it also included local enterprises, regional forces, and groups dedicated to a vast assortment of issues including gender and profit. According to Leslie, colleges were subject to "urbanization and industrialization that created forces that challenged the local and denominational groups that had founded colleges."[54] His is one of the only works that clearly places local boosterism and religious groups on equal footing in the founding of colleges.

The Influence of Philanthropy

The booster spirit, as it took hold and flourished, led to a concern for community that fostered a new peculiarly American institution, public philanthropy. The institutionalization of the public philanthropic spirit in the nineteenth century led to the founding and sustaining of many colleges in the United States. Although the booster movement has been inexorably linked to financial investments, people of wealth increasingly turned to the community and its institutions, or its emerging institutions, to effect change through a large philanthropic gift. Boorstin identified Benjamin Franklin as the patron saint of American philanthropy and summed up his philosophy, saying:

For Franklin, doing good was not a private act between bountiful giver and grateful receiver; it was prudent social act. A wise act of philanthropy that would sooner or later benefit the giver along with other members of the community. While living in Philadelphia, Franklin developed philanthropic enterprises which included projects for establishing a city police, for paving and better cleaning and lighting of city streets, for a circulating library, for the American Philosophical Society for Useful Knowledge, for an Academy for the Education of Youth (origin of The University of Pennsylvania), for a debating society and a fire department.[55]

Philanthropy has taken a multiplicity of forms throughout history. Understanding philanthropy in specific times and places develops our understanding of the different roles philanthropy has played in society in general and higher education in particular. The modern notion of philanthropy began with Andrew Carnegie, who, in an essay titled *The Gospel of Wealth* published in 1889,[56] gave birth to the idea that the rich should establish public trusts in lieu of passing their riches to their children. Other industrialists of the day such as Rockefeller, Vanderbilt, and Hopkins followed Carnegie's lead, and their so-called *philanthropic boosts* not only improved dire social situations but also created institutions of higher education. Heidelberg College and Tiffin University, albeit on a much smaller scale, would later benefit from their own philanthropic boosts.

End Notes

1 Paul F. Grendler, *The Universities of the Italian Renaissance* (Baltimore: Johns Hopkins University Press, 2002).

2 Roger L. Geiger, *The American College in the Nineteenth Century, Vanderbilt Issues in Higher Education* (Nashville: Vanderbilt University Press, 2000).

3 Ibid., 5.

4 Ibid., 140.

5 Michael A. Grandillo, "Fraternities and Sororities," in *Encyclopedia of Education, 2nd Ed.*, ed. James W. Guthrie (New York: MacMillan, 2002).

6 Laurence R. Veysey, *The Emergence of the American University* (Chicago: University of Chicago Press, 1965), 264–268; Sandra Oleson and John Voss, *The Organization of Knowledge in America, 1860–1920* (Baltimore: Johns Hopkins University Press, 1978); and Roger Geiger, *Research & Relevant Knowledge: American Research Universities since World War II, Transaction Series in Higher Education* (New Brunswick, N.J.: Transaction Publishers, 2004).

7 Ibid., 152.

8 Charles B. Flood, *Lee: The Last Years* (Boston: Houghton Mifflin Company, 1981).

9 Ernest P. Earnest, *Academic Procession: An Informal History of the American College, 1636 to 1953* (Indianapolis: Bobbs-Merrill, 1953).

10 Ibid., 129.

11 John Seiler Brubacher and Willis Rudy, *Higher Education in Transition: A History of American Colleges and Universities, 1636–1968* (New York: Harper & Row, 1968).

12 Veysey, *The Emergence of the American University*.

13 United States Census Bureau, *The Census of the United States of America, 1890.* The United States Census Bureau website (www.census.gov) is also very helpful.

14 Paul Van Riper, *History of the United States Civil Service* (Evanston, Ill.: Row, Peterson, 1958).

15 James Herbert Siward Bossard, J. Frederic Dewhurst, and The Wharton School, *University Education for Business; A Study of Existing Needs and Practices* (Philadelphia: University of Pennsylvania Press, 1931).

16 Lee C. Deighton, *The Encyclopedia of Education*, Vol. 1 (New York: Macmillan, 1971), 510.

17 Benjamin R. Haynes and Harry P. Jackson, *A History of Business Education in the United States* (New York: Southwestern Publishing Company, 1935), 7–8.

18 John Mair, *Bookeeping Methodized: A Methodical Treatise on Merchant Accounts According to the Italian Form* (Edinburgh: W. Sands, A. Murray, and J. Cockran, 1737).

19 Thomas Dilworth, *The Schoolmaster's Assistant: Being a Compendium of Arithmetic, both Practical and Theoretical* (London: Henry Kent, 1768).

20 Benjamin Workman, *The American Accountant* (Philadelphia: William Young, 1796).

21 Charles Reigner, "Beginnings of the Commercial Schools," *Education* 42 (November, 1921).

22 Jay W. Miller, *The Independent Business School in American Education* (New York: McGraw-Hill, 1964).

23 Cloyd Heck Marvin, *Commercial Education in Secondary Schools* (New York: Henry Holt and Company, 1922), 14.

24 Charles G. Reigner, "Notes for a History of Commercial Education," *The Rowe Budget XXXI* (October, 1929): 4–5.

25 Ellwood P. Cubberley, *History of Education: Educational Practice and Progress Considered as a Phase of the Development and Spread of Western Civilization* (Boston: Houghton Mifflin, 1920), 791.

26 Leon Carroll Marshall, *The Collegiate School of Business: Its Status at the Close of the First Quarter of the Twentieth Century* (Chicago: University of Chicago Press, 1928), 3.

27 Michael W. Sedlak and Harold F. Williamson, *The Evolution of Management Education: A History of the Northwestern University J. L. Kellogg Graduate School of Management, 1908–1983* (Champaign: University of Illinois Press, 1983), 4.

28 Marshall, *The Collegiate School of Business*, 4.

29 E. W. Barnhart, "Early Beginnings of Commercial Education," *Vocational Education Magazine* (October, 1922): 101.

30 Paul Monroe, *A Cyclopedia of Education*, Vol. 2 (New York: The Macmillan Company, 1911).

31 Ibid., 11.

32 Ibid., 144.

33 C. L. Knight, G. J. Previts, and T. A. Ratcliffe, *A Reference Chronology of Events Significant to the Development of Accountancy in the United States* (Tuscaloosa, Ala.: The Academy of Accounting, Monograph 1, 1976).

34 Luca Pacioli, *Summa de Arithmetica, Geometria, Proporti-oni, et Portionalita* (Venice: Pagininus, 1494).

35 James O Winjum, *The Role of Accounting in the Economic Development of England, 1500–1750* (Urbana, Ill.: Center for International Education and Research in Accounting, 1978).

36 William Mitchell, *A New and Complete System of Bookkeeping* (Philadelphia: Bioren and Madan, 1796).

37 Thomas Turner, *An Epitome of Bookkeeping by Double Entry* (Portland, Maine: Printed by Jenks and Shirley, for Thomas Clark, 1804).

38 James A. Bennett, *The American System of Practical Bookkeeping* (New York: Collins and Hannay, 1826).

39 Tamara Plakins Thornton, *Handwriting in America: A Cultural History* (New Haven, Conn.: Yale University Press, 1996).

40 Ibid., 6.

41 James Henry Lewis, *The Best Method of Pen-Making Illustrated by Practical Observations on the Art of Writing, to Which Are Added, Directions for Holding the Pen Properly, and Many Other Secrets Worth Knowing, to Those Who Wish to Write Well* (Manchester: Printed for the author, 1825), 32.

42 George Fisher, *The American Instructor: Or Young Man's Best Companion* (Philadelphia: Fisher, 1748).

43 Thornton, *Handwriting in America*, 48.

44 Ibid., 49.

45 "The Educational Use of the Typewriter," in *Education* (April, 1902).

46 D. Appleton, *Appletons' Annual Cyclopedia and Register of Important Events: Embracing Political, Military, and Ecclesiastical Affairs; Public Documents; Biography, Statistics, Commerce, Finance, Literature, Science, Agriculture, and Mechanical Industry*, Vol. XV (New York: D. Appleton and Company, 1890), 807–818.

47 History of the Remington Company (www.remington.com).

48 Daniel J. Boorstin, *The Americans: The Colonial Experience* (New York: Random House, 1958); and Daniel J. Boorstin, *The Americans: The Democratic Experience* (New York: Random House, 1973).

49 Daniel. J. Boorstin, *Hidden Histories: Exploring Our Secret Past* (New York: Random House, 1995), 194.

50 Ibid.

51 Ibid., 195.

52 *The Compact Oxford English Dictionary* (Oxford: Oxford Press, 1991).

53 William Leslie, *Gentleman and Scholars: College and Community in the Age of the University, 1865–1917* (University Park: The Pennsylvania State University Press, 1992), xv.

54 Ibid., 1.

55 Boorstin, *Hidden Histories*, 204.

56 Steven J. Ott, *The Nature of the Nonprofit Sector* (Boulder, Colo.: Westview Press, 2001).

{Bustling downtown Tiffin in the Roaring Twenties. Courtesy of the Seneca County Museum.}

Chapter 2

Ohio and
Higher Education

The Ohio Country was the epicenter of competing forces in the 1700s. Historically claimed by the Iroquois Nation since their ousting of the Eries in the mid-seventeenth century, the region was officially claimed by the French in 1669. French explorer La Salle[1] was the first European to see the Ohio River, and the first written history of Ohio came from the Jesuits.[2] Defined by the Great Lake to the north and the Great River to the south, the region took its name from its famed tributary: *la belle riviere*, beautiful river in La Salle's vernacular or the Iroquoian *O-y-o* or *O-he-yo*, which became Ohio.

Soon, the British Empire and her settlers along the Atlantic seaboard, long separated from the Ohio Country by the Appalachian Mountains, began to look inward for new lands and more control of the fur trade. Settlers from the nearby colonies of Virginia and Pennsylvania introduced more competitive trading practices to the Native Americans, breaking French domination of the fur trade.[3] This conflict between the French and British in the New World was a part of a century-long struggle for worldwide domination (sometimes referred to as the Second One Hundred Years' War, 1689–1763). Colonial fights in North America for imperial and mercantile supremacy mirrored separate but related wars around the globe. By the middle of the eighteenth century, Ohio was drawn into these battles.

While the economies of Native American peoples had long been influenced by trade with Europeans for fur and skins, the conflict between the French and the British forced the tribes into closer relationships with the Europeans. Their fight for land control and trade forced the Indians into wary compacts with both colonial powers, bringing cultural and ecological change. Ohio's strategic place and the economic importance of the fur trade made it the continent's most coveted possession.

Apart from the problem of navigating an increasingly hostile environment brought about by the confrontation of French and British forces, Native Americans' growing dependence on the fur trade gradually changed their way of life. Over-hunting of the land, coupled with their reliance on a single-trading commodity, contributed to their loss of self-sufficiency. Unable to master the production of their own weapons and iron goods, they became more and more dependent upon French and British traders and their more sophisticated technology.

By 1750, Ohio stood at the midpoint of New France,

which ranged from Canada to the Gulf of Mexico; the strong colonies of the British Empire lay to the east. Christopher Gist returned to Virginia from a seven-month tour of Ohio and encouraged the Ohio Land Company to begin a settlement. George Washington's subsequent mission to oust the French was repulsed. The issue as to who would settle the Ohio Country was finally decided by the French and Indian War, or the Seven Year War (1753–1763), when Great Britain, with the support of their North American colonies and Native Americans, fought the French and their Native American allies for control of the American interior and the Ohio Valley. The British conquest of Fort Duquesne (renamed Fort Pitt) and later Montreal ended the war. The Treaty of Paris of 1763 ended French power in North America and gave control of Ohio to the British.

As the treaty was being signed in Paris, however, Indians, led by Pontiac, formed a confederation to protect their lands passing to British hands. Pontiac sought to remove the British through a series of attacks, forcing the British to respond with a Royal Proclamation in 1763 that directed colonists to stay east of the Alleghenies and the Indians to the west. A patrol force, funded by new taxes, would keep the peace. The closure of the frontier to the colonists, new taxation without representation, and potential loss of the fur trade was not the

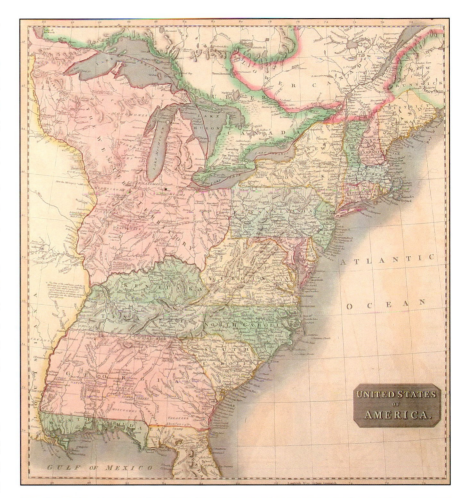

{An 1817 map of the United States of America, which included the Northwest Territory. The Larry H. Christman Collection.}

Early Cartography Depicting the Western Territories as Ohio Moves to Statehood

Most American maps of the period were printed in large atlases and originated in Europe, especially Great Britain and France. The scale and accuracy developed slowly while natural, geographical, and political lines became more defined. The early nineteenth-century maps became more exact with the application of scientific methods, although the dates of the maps usually represented an earlier time. Mapmaking was not perfected until the advent of aerial photography in the 1920s.

The United States of America, John Melish. Philadelphia: Mathew Carey and Son, 1820. The Whitney Telle Collection, Tuscaloosa, Alabama, and Courtesy of the University of Alabama Map Library, Craig Remington.

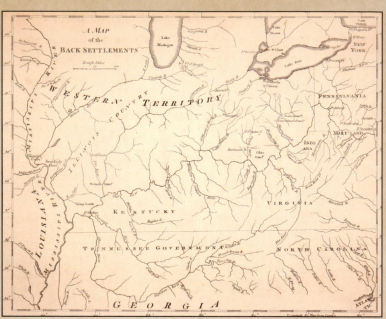

The Map of the Back Settlements. The American Geography by Jeddah Morse. London: John Stockdale, 1794. The Larry H. Christman Collection.

A map of the Northern Part of the United States of America. The Wayne Treaty Line of 1795 is also shown. C. Dilly, 1798. The Larry H. Christman Collection.

Early Cartography Depicting the Development of Ohio

Map of the State of Ohio, 1820. Drawn by James Kilbourne, published by E. Windsor, Connecticut, 1820. The Larry H. Christman Collection.

The first separately issued map of the state of Ohio, by Rufus Putnam, January 1804. The Larry H. Christman Collection.

Early county lines of Ohio and Indian reserved Lands in the Black Swamp, 1818, John Melish. Philadelphia: Mathew Carey and Son, 1820. The Whitney Telle Collection, Tuscaloosa, Alabama, and Courtesy of the University of Alabama Map Library, Craig Remington.

outcome the colonists imagined from the French and Indian War. Although the goals of the proclamation were never realized, the war and the British actions thereafter increased colonial hostility toward the British government, moving toward independence. The American Revolutionary War followed with the Ohio Indians on the British side. Settlers of Ohio would continue to have to deal with hostile Native Americans until well into the 1800s.

Toward Statehood

At the end of the American Revolution, the Northwest Territory was granted to the United States by the Treaty of Paris of 1783. Immediately, discussions ensued on how to settle the territory and provide an orderly entry into the Union. Ratification of the Articles of Confederation was delayed by contested land claims in the territory. Settling these differences was important since the new nation hoped to use land sales as a source of funding. Thomas Jefferson's vision of an *Empire of Liberty* between the Alleghenies and the Mississippi would begin to be realized with a series of land ordinances passed by Congress beginning in 1784.

The Land Ordinance of 1785 called for survey provisions creating ranges and townships in a grid pattern to facilitate land purchases and ownerships, setting a minimum auction price of $640 an acre. The high cost prohibited many individuals from affording land, giving rise to land speculators and stock companies (the Ohio Company and the Symmes Purchase Group) buying land in large tracts. They subsequently broke up the large tracts, selling small sections, at large profits, to settlers. The population grew accordingly. The Northwest Ordinance of 1787 established a path to statehood and gave its new inhabitants rights and freedoms not yet guaranteed in the original states, privileges later defined in the Bill of Rights.

The American government quickly moved to hold the land by appointing Arthur St. Clair governor of the Northwest Territory. This ardent federalist wielded a heavy hand in Ohio's development in the 1790s. Finding, upon his arrival at Marietta in 1788, an Indian population angered by broken treaties and promises and a territory where the British still held forts, St. Clair only added to the hostilities through diplomatic blunders and an overbearing manner.

St. Clair's inability to forge a peace forced the Washington Administration to take military action. Josiah Harmar was chosen to lead an expedition north from Cincinnati to present-day Fort Wayne. Harmar's campaign was soundly defeated by the Indians on October 21, 1790, forcing Washington to replace him with St. Clair. Embarking on a plan to build forts twenty-five miles apart to help ensure victory, St. Clair sought to follow Harmar's route with better men and supplies. He too failed. Little Turtle of the Miamis and Blue Jacket of the Shawnees easily disposed of St. Clair in a battle at modern-day Mercer County. The Mohawks' vision espoused by Joseph Brant of a sovereign Indian nation in the Northwest was closer to fruition, and Washington's hold on the west was threatened.

With the Indians gaining ground and St. Clair defeated, Washington turned to a proven Revolutionary War hero, Anthony Wayne. The British held Fort Miami near Toledo, and the Indians still desired peace. Learning of Harmar's and St. Clair's failures, Wayne methodically and strategically trained twenty-five hundred troops and scouts on how to defeat the Indians. Better funded by Congress and trained in Indian warfare, Wayne's army headed north in 1792 from Fort Washington in Cincinnati. He built forts with meaningful names at the site where St. Clair was defeated, *Recovery,* and deeper into Indian Territory, *Defiance.* Wayne defeated the Indians led by Blue Jacket in the Battle of Fallen Timbers on the banks of the Maumee River, persuading the British to give up their support for the Native Americans. Wayne immediately called a meeting at Fort Greene Ville (Darke County) in June of 1795 to discuss peace. At the talks, attended by more than eleven hundred Native Americans and lasting two months, Wayne, who was well respected by the Indians, effected a significant peace treaty. The Treaty of Greenville granted much of northwest and north-central Ohio to the Indians, preserving land and water routes. Sixteen years of relative peace ensued.

The Treaty of Greenville made settlement in Ohio less precarious. Immigrants from the east poured into Ohio. There followed a growing movement for statehood. St. Clair, as governor of the new territory, resisted statehood. He opposed a census, which would determine future statehood, and a sensible division of the territory into prospective states. Holding fast to federalist and aristocratic views, St. Clair endeared himself to no one except President Adams and eastern elites. Federalist ideas about government were not in concert with frontier realities in the Northwest Territory. Jeffersonians found Ohio fertile ground for practical experimentation in state building, and new frontier leaders found Jefferson's republican ideals appealing for the new state. William H. Harrison and Thomas Worthington opposed St. Clair, and together they pushed through Congress the Division Act of 1800, which carved out Ohio from the territory in preparation for statehood. Chillicothe was made the seat of government in the east; Vincennes, the western capital. Worthington's resistance to Governor St. Clair earned him the title "Father of Ohio Statehood," and he along with his physician and brother-in-law, Edward Tiffin, would shape early Ohio.

With President Adams's support, St. Clair was able to remain governor even while his popularity waned and Jeffersonian ideals took hold in Ohio. By 1800, the requisite sixty thousand population needed for statehood was present. And although St. Clair tried dividing the territory again so as to avoid meeting the threshold, the election of Jefferson in that year and the work of Worthington in Congress stymied St. Clair, and the path to statehood became clear.

On November 1, 1802, Ohio's Constitutional Convention was called in Chillicothe. A young band of Chillicothians, led by Worthington and Tiffin, along with Nathaniel Massie and Michael Baldwin, were imbued with Jeffersonian ideals. Their zeal and organization won them twenty-six of the thirty-five delegates to the convention, assuring statehood and defeat of St. Clair's federalism in Ohio. In less than a month, a twenty-page Constitution was passed and sent via Worthington to Congress. Ohio was made a state on February 19, 1803.

Edward Tiffin became Ohio's first governor, with Chillicothe the state's capital. Tiffin ably managed the dissimilar New Englanders and Virginians who populated the northern and southern parts of the state, respectively. Tiffin's energetic and sensible dealing with the volatile Aaron Burr expedition won the praise of President Jefferson. It was a time of rapid growth and relative peace: the population grew from 45,000 in 1800 to more than 230,000 by 1810.[4] To coincide with the population explosion, the fledgling state's infrastructure needed to be secured, most notably education and transportation.

HON. EDWARD TIFFIN
First Governor of Ohio, After Whom Tiffin was Named

Transportation and Higher Education in Ohio

True provincialism for Ohio is a political not a geographical entity, as its eastern and western boundaries were determined by prearranged states and its northern and southern parameters by bodies of water. Therefore, the political and cultural forces played an important factor in the state's development. Along the way, improvements in transportation and communication accelerated development. Consequently, from the beginning, accessibility has been the keynote of Ohio's history.

Ohio's location contributed much to its own development. As the easternmost state in the Midwest, it served populations in markets east and west from its combination of natural and manmade transportation systems. As commerce on the Great Lakes developed in the 1840s, Ohio responded by completing canals connecting to the Ohio River.[5] During the canal era, Ohio's system of artificial waterways furnished links to natural lakes and rivers connecting New York City to New Orleans at the mouth of the Mississippi River. Ohio's rapid development between 1830 and 1850 owes much to this factor.

The quick development of education in Ohio was a response to the rise in population and commerce during the 1830s and 1840s. Eastern businessmen

{The Honorable Edward Tiffin. Tiffin, Ohio, was named after Ohio's first governor, Edward Tiffin. The founders of Tiffin University took the name of their city, further memorializing his name.}

reached out to newly created western markets with accessible transportation. Commerce flourished and the increased distribution of goods in the region called for new recourses for communication and trained labor. As Americans and industry expanded, so did the need for improved business techniques, especially in accounting and other specialized clerical tasks.

As a part of the Northwest Ordinance of 1787, Ohio was destined for cultivation by religious education. Education was praised, but not endowed, in the statement "Religion, morality and knowledge, being necessary for good government and the happiness of mankind, schools and the means of educating shall forever be encouraged."[6] The true history of the development of Ohio's independent college, moreover, is framed by American society—its life, its politics, and its cultural forces—and the reflection of these forces in a microcosm. These are sagas of localities, states, and the nation.

The Northwest Ordinance, coupled with the ensuing State Constitution of 1803, which stated that "schools and the means of instruction shall forever be encouraged by legislative provisions,"[7] provided fertile ground for religious groups and localities. Charters for colleges and universities were required from the state legislature and obtained quite easily. This easy chartering was further augmented at the local level when the state gave chartering power to the county auditors in 1852, thus increasing the local control of college founding.[8] According to Eugene H. Roseboom, in *The History of Ohio*:

Ohio was overblessed with institutions of higher learning by 1851, but the legislature invited the creation of new ones by general law in 1852 governing such incorporations. It permitted any group of five or more individuals to incorporate as a college or university by proving to the satisfaction of the county auditor that the proposed corporation had property of the value of $550.00. They might elect a board, a president, and a faculty and go into the business of granting degrees. No state supervision was required.[9]

These governmental developments made the formation and founding of colleges in Ohio easy. Many were incorporated, but many failed. These chartered colleges played more of a role in spurring the growth of high-school-equivalent academies. There were 3,873 students, of which 2,157 were enrolled at the academy level in the state's twenty-two colleges in 1859.[10] This allowed local boosters the opportunity to develop these new institutions into stronger colleges. The field of higher education in Ohio, for most of the nineteenth century, was left to the private province of the religious and local boosters. Public support of higher education in Ohio was nearly completely absent, except for the nominal support of Ohio University, Miami University, and Wilberforce.

Even after passage of the Morrill Act in 1862, the Ohio General Assembly was so deeply split on how to respond to taxation issues and the effects they would have on existing institutions, that the bill to create the Ohio Agriculture and Mechanical College did not pass until 1871. This institution later came to be called The Ohio State University. Nevertheless, the Morrill Act and the founding of this land grant university in Columbus had little effect on the landscape of higher education in Ohio until the next century, according to Alexis Cope, who wrote the first official *History of The Ohio State University* in 1920.[11]

Canals, in the early 1800s, were considered the chief means in Ohio for improving accessibility and transportation. Securing adequate canals, coupled with roads, was important to the success of Ohio and its emerging towns, and in the future of its colleges. For example, canals and roads were a significant reason for the Congregationalists' selection of Hudson, Ohio, as the location of Western Reserve College.[12] These waterways later competed with the network of railroads. Both means of transportation spread throughout the state until there was scarcely a village more than a few miles away from a canal or railroad.[13]

More than any other mode of transportation, the railroad epitomized the power of American technological and commercial development. The advent of the railroad advanced economic, cultural, social, and political development of the United States in the nineteenth century. The impact of the railroad on education is often overlooked but equally important. The railroad proved to be a great asset to the development of the college, and the rapid development of the railroad and colleges mirrored each other, especially

{Trains and interurbans played a major role in Tiffin's early development and growth. Tiffin was early in receiving rail service; the Mad River and Lake Erie reached Tiffin in 1841. Interurbans, shown here, connected Tiffin with other cities. The Tiffin, Fostoria and Eastern Electric Railway provided interurban transportation from the 1890s to well into the 1920s. Courtesy of the Seneca County Museum.}

{Left: Perry Street Bridge}

{Below left: Tiffin Railroad Depot. Courtesy of the Seneca County Museum.}

in Ohio. John Stover's *American Railroad*[14] illustrates the dominance of the flourishing of track in Ohio: "The center of population, which in 1810 had been but a few miles from Washington, D.C. had moved by the eve of the Civil War to a spot west of Athens, Ohio,"[15] and by "1860, Ohio was first in railroad mileage in the nation."[16] It is clear that the acceleration of the settlement and agricultural output of the western two-thirds of the United States was strikingly influenced by the advent of the railroad.[17]

However, railroads developed in a peculiar way in America. In contrast with England, where railroads developed to carry people from one established town to another, American railroads were sent out into the frontier West. "Nineteenth century America had seen the booster railroad arise to match the booster press, the booster college and the upstart town."[18] Therefore, the American booster railroad and the American college had similar beginnings, as they were commonly built in the hope "they would be called into being by the population they would serve."[19] In addition, in Ohio, the railroads and the colleges arrived at about the same time. Along with prematurely built grand hotels, town boosters sought railroads and colleges in an anticipatory and upside-down fashion. Nevertheless, this developing infrastructure would create a powerful educational apparatus for Ohio higher education.

The railroad and the college have a lot in common. The quick development of colleges and the rapid development of railroads in America were also born out of the same legal structure: The Dartmouth Case of 1819 gave both railroads and the colleges the right to independent control of corporations and freedom from direct control of the state. In *Passage to Union: How the Railroad Transformed American Life, 1829–1929*,[20] Sarah H. Gordon states the Dartmouth Case was as equally important to the railroad as it was to the independent college, declaring "that charters did not imply a monopoly, and not invariably act in public interest."[21]

The presence of a railroad was a major factor in deciding the location of many colleges. The president of Heidelberg College, the Reverend George W. Williard, D.D., remarking that Tiffin was the best choice available because of its population and railroad, said in 1879 that "we can see the wisdom evidenced in the selection of Tiffin . . . it has grown more rapidly and has railroad facilities which neither of the other places

has. It has an intelligent and enterprising population of 10,000 inhabitants and it is beautifully situated on the banks of the Sandusky River, which runs through it."[22] Even after Heidelberg College selected the town, transportation played a role in the location of the college within the city borders as well. Reverend Schully, who was instrumental in securing a college for Tiffin, jocularly remarked that the Mad River and Lake Erie Railroad—the first to be built in the state—and the Sandusky River ran near the site on which the college now stands. The site was selected so that if the college did not succeed "it might be more easily placed on the cars and shipped to some other place."[23] The early leaders of the college sought to be an outgrowth of the community by adapting the course of study to the wants of the community, opening its doors to women, and appealing to prospective students outside the Reformed Church.

State Policy of Chartering Colleges in Ohio

The *laissez-faire* policy toward the development of colleges and universities by Ohio's lawmakers during the first 125 years of statehood served the founders of the future Tiffin University well. For the most part, Ohio legislatures left the development of higher education institutions to strong local boosters and spirited religious leaders. From 1803 to the Legislative Act of 1882, colleges and universities were required to receive their charters by legislative action. After the passage of the Legislative Act, charters were secured through the county auditor and could be granted to corporations of not less than five persons who held the purpose of founding a university or college. These individuals could elect themselves as trustees, select a president, and appoint a faculty. Very few limitations were placed on these newly formed institutions, although the capital assets needed were slowly increased from five hundred dollars in 1872 to twenty-five thousand dollars by 1908. In 1880, the General Assembly of Ohio gave the power of incorporation to the Ohio secretary of state, and the meager requirements for chartering continued for colleges and universities. Once approved, a college or university could confer any degree that was awarded by an "institution of similar name anywhere in the U.S." In 1914, the authority for degree confirmation in the state of Ohio was passed on to the superintendent of public instruction.[24]

Ohio's Institutions of Higher Learning

Due to the relative ease of chartering a college in Ohio, the state saw many institutions come and go. Currently, Ohio is home to 152 institutions of higher education: 14 four-year public universities; 57 two-year university branch campuses, community colleges, and technical colleges; and 74 baccalaureate-granting independent colleges and universities. Founded in 1804, Ohio University was the first institution of higher learning in Ohio and the Northwest Territory. Originally called American Western University, the college is located in Athens, Ohio. Miami University in Oxford followed; although chartered in 1809 it did not enroll students until 1823. Ohio's first private, de-

nominational college, Kenyon College in Gambier, was founded by Episcopalians in 1824.

Colleges and universities formed in the nineteenth century were religious, social, and economic endeavors. The denominational spirit was alive, but not always well; although almost every existing religion in the new west of Ohio founded a college, few survived. Eighty colleges failed and thirty-five were chartered that never opened.[25] They did, however, reflect the uniqueness of their region, the distinctiveness of their denominations, as well as the academic demands placed upon them. These factors gave us diverse institutions: from the Swedenborgians of Urbana to the Marianists of Dayton; from the Campbellites of Hiram to the Quakers of Malone and Wilmington. Ohio's colleges and universities represented important social movements, including women's education at Lake Erie and Western College; African-American education at Wilberforce; and coeducation and early non-discriminate enrollment practices at Oberlin. The unique educational pasts of Ohio's colleges also tell us about the contributions of for-profit education: Ohio Northern as a normal school, Franklin and Tiffin as business, and a variety of for-profit medical, dental, and law schools. Many of today's surviving colleges started as secondary academies before offering degrees.

Few higher education sagas are more dramatic than the story of Case Western Reserve University.[26] This institutional history has many of Ohio's college-founding forces wrapped into one institution: how two very different small colleges, one religious, one not, in different locations, through their responses to societal and economic forces, emerged to rank as one of the nation's elite research universities. From a variety of mergers, site changes, political struggles, curriculum innovations, philanthropic boosts, and later a federation, we now have the modern Case Western Reserve University in Cleveland, Ohio. All of the unique stories of Ohio's colleges and universities reach back to the earliest brief glimmer of origin to settle on a founding or establishment date.

FORT BALL.

Tiffin and Seneca County, Ohio, and Higher Education

Tiffin, Ohio, and Seneca County grew and developed together in Northwest Ohio on the edge of the Great Black Swamp. A little west of the center of the county, along the Sandusky River, amid a thick forest, rose two communities: Fort Ball on the west bank of the river and Tiffin on the east. Although growth was slow until the railroad first appeared in 1841, vigorous local boosters began to claim lands and develop their new communities. Fort Ball started as a military post built to support the War of 1812 efforts and the stockades and garrisons along the Sandusky River, especially Fort Seneca nine miles north and Fort Stephenson (Fremont). In July 1813, Lieutenant Colonel James Ball built a fort—originally called Camp Ball—large enough to hold five hundred men.[27] Erastus Bowe led the first authenticated settlement by a non-native and arrived in Fort Ball on November 18, 1817. Bowe built a log house and operated the first tavern in Seneca County. The building was located on the northwest corner of North Washington Street and Frost Parkway. The area of present-day downtown Tiffin was purchased by Josiah Hedges in 1821, who named the streets after early presidents and the city after his Jeffersonian friend, Edward Tiffin. Hedges's town struggled compared to Fort Ball until the land office was relocated to Tiffin from Delaware in 1828.[28]

Seneca County's boundaries were determined after the first U.S. survey in the early 1820s, and Seneca was organized as an independent county of the state of Ohio on April 1, 1820. However, it took four years for the General Assembly of Ohio to pass an enabling act on January 22, 1824, officially recognizing Seneca County as a separate and distinct political subdivision

PIONEER BUILDINGS

1778 · JOSIAH HEDGES · 1858

FOUNDER

TIFFIN, OHIO, 1821

...T TAVERN, BUILT IN 1817

FIRST COURT HOUSE, BUIL...

FORT BALL, BUILT IN 1813

...BRICK BUILDING, BUILT IN 1824

FIRST PROTESTANT CHURCH, BUILT I...

{Josiah Hedges (April 9, 1778–July 15, 1858). The founder of Tiffin, Ohio, was a quintessential local booster. His land grant and his assistance in raising funds ensured Heidelberg College would be located in his upstart town.}

of Ohio.[29] In the meantime, the General Assembly, in the winter of 1822, appointed three commissioners to organize a county government. The state called for the county's first elections of sheriff and coroner, and commissions to be held in April 1824 when the act of the assembly took effect.[30]

The Sagacity of Josiah Hedges

William Lang, noted nineteenth-century Seneca County historian, credits the ascendency of Tiffin as a thriving urban area to the *Sagacity of Josiah Hedges*.

Seneca County "settled more rapidly than any other county in northwestern Ohio"[31] and Hedges's foresight, discernment, and keen judgment made Tiffin and Seneca County take off while similar upstart communities were left behind. More than 125 years later, contemporary historians would echo Lang's observations: Charles Glaab, known as one of America's outstanding urban historians, said Hedges's entrepreneurship and boosterism is representative of what happened in successful cities across the West.[32] Enlightened self-interest combined with adroit decision making and political maneu-

{Flood waters at Perry Street and South Washington Street looking north. Tiffin did not escape the Great Flood of 1913, known as Ohio's most significant natural disaster. Rainfall from March 23–27 averaged 6 to 11 inches a day, the death toll was 467, and more than 40,000 homes were damaged or destroyed statewide. Dayton was the most severely struck, with 14 square miles of the city under water. Ohio's cities had to take bold, progressive action to stop future flooding. Tiffin, like Dayton, did and their response has stopped central city flooding for almost 100 years. Courtesy of the Seneca County Museum and Jeremy Croy.}

{Early schools of higher learning in Seneca County. Clockwise from top:

College of the Ursuline Sisters. In 1921 at the request of Bishop Schrembs, the first Bishop of Toledo, the Sisters switched the college to a Catholic co-educational high school. Calvert High School was opened in 1923 under then Bishop and later Cardinal Samuel Stritch.

The Seneca County Academy, an early normal school in Republic, Ohio.

The Fostoria Academy, the campus's signature building was quite similar to College Hall at Heidelberg.}

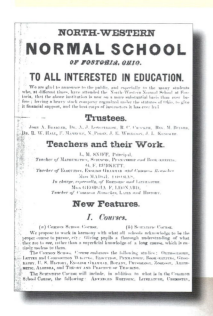

vering, allowing Hedges to survive the slow economy of the mid-nineteenth century and be positioned to create local markets to weather national financial storms. Tiffin, not unlike Ohio's larger cities, had no other choice than to respond to financial ups and downs with new vigor. The time between 1848 and 1854, which historian Carl Abbot calls "an era of decision for almost every American city of the Middle West,"[33] was a time when cities began to realized that commercial opportunities should be seized upon and exploited to secure growth. Josiah Hedges understood these times and sought to add a college to his portfolio of city amenities.

Hedges commissioned his brother, General James Hedges, to survey and plat the new town of Tiffin. Josiah owned or controlled the majority of land in central Seneca County, which he developed into the city of Tiffin. Housing tracts, parks, and roads were laid out with his blessing as he used his political influence to secure railroads, government work, investors in commerce, and Tiffin as the county seat. His community improvements and investments permeated every aspect of the newly formed city. For example, Hedges built and owned the first bridge in Tiffin; he charged two dollars for a year's worth of passage. He was the consummate local booster, and he later would secure a college for his emerging city.

Edward Tiffin and Josiah Hedges's close friendship served Hedges well. Both Fort Ball and Tiffin vied for the seat of justice after the state formally recognized Seneca County. Friendly rivalries turned to hostilities during the selection process after Tiffin was chosen over Fort Ball. Interestingly, Fort Ball's proposed site for the courthouse is the present location of Tiffin University's campus. Hedges eventually brokered a peace between the two communities by purchasing the financial interest of Fort Ball boosters. Tiffin, Ohio, was incorporated on March 7, 1835. Together, Tiffin and Seneca County quickly grew:

The population in Seneca County Ohio grew from 5,139 in 1830 to 30,827 in 1860. Settlers east of the Sandusky River were primarily from southern Ohio, New York, Pennsylvania and Maryland while immigrants, mainly Germans and Irish settled west of the river. This steady population growth slowed in the 1860s, with half the males between 18 and 48 gone serving in the Civil War.[34]

As Tiffin and Seneca County grew and prospered, institutions of higher education began to emerge. In addition to Heidelberg College, normal and commercial colleges served the area. Both Fostoria, Ohio (sixteen miles northwest of Tiffin), and Republic, Ohio (nine miles east of Tiffin), were served by normal colleges. The Northwestern Normal School of Fostoria was founded in 1875 as a "heavy stock company, organized under the statutes of Ohio, to give financial support, and the best instructors."[35] It was owned by prominent leaders of Fostoria and eventually added commercial training. Fostoria Academy, founded by the Presbyterians in 1858 in Fostoria, struggled to survive the Civil War. However, they managed to build a substantial building in 1879 and continued under different leadership and ownership and, at one time,

{Downtown Tiffin, with the Remmele Building in the background flying a flag. Courtesy of the Seneca County Museum.}

operated rather successfully as Ohio Normal College into the early 1900s. The Northwest Normal School in Republic was a successful normal school in the late 1800s and was a chief educator of local teachers in the latter part of the nineteenth century. The school is best known for its mathematics instructor, Henry Baker Brown. Brown left the normal school in 1873 and founded the Northern Indiana Normal and Business School in Valparaiso on September 16, 1873. This institution developed into Valparaiso University, and Brown is considered its founder.[36]

The Ursuline Sisters provided the first form of commercial education in Seneca County. In 1863, the Sisters founded the College of the Ursuline Sisters[37] in Tiffin, on the southeast corner of Jefferson and Madison Streets, and operated both as an academy and a college.

{An early photo of downtown Tiffin. Courtesy of the Seneca County Museum.}

The college was located in their convent. That site is now the campus of Calvert High School, which they also helped found. The Sisters were aggressive marketers and committed to commercial education. They competed favorably with Heidelberg for local students.

The College of the Ursuline Sisters was under the leadership of Sister Liguori Superior. The Sisters advertised to offer "the best advantages in every department of education"[38] and the College was open to both day and boarding pupils. The scholastic year for boarding students was divided into two five-month sessions, which began on the first Monday in September and February. The day scholars' year was divided into four quarter-terms of eleven weeks. However, pupils were received at any time and completed on a rolling instructional basis. As time went on, the College of the

Ursuline Sisters increasingly emphasized commercial education, particularly bookkeeping, stenography, and later typewriting. The instruction of the college was comprehensive and provided a wide range of subjects for the day. The variety of progressive offerings included painting, music, and drawing, as well as elocution and a liberal offering of modern and classical languages. The citizens of Tiffin, Ohio, have been served by the Ursuline Sisters continuously since 1863, and they are still participating in the education of its young people today.[39]

Heidelberg College in the Nineteenth Century

The Ohio Synod of the German Reformed Church sought to establish a seminary in Ohio as early as 1833. The Synod needed trained ministers to serve newly formed Ohio congregations and an anticipated demand for Reformed Church ministers in a burgeoning western frontier, due to German immigration to Ohio. After three failed starts in sixteen years, the Synod decided it would be more practicable if they would combine their vision for a seminary with a classical college. On October 4, 1849, the Synod voted to establish a committee with the charge of "soliciting proposals from different localities looking toward the permanent location of an institution."[40] The committee went about its task to secure a location with vigor

and energy. A clarion call went out to cities and villages, through the Synod's network of congregations in Ohio, to present their best proposals and financial inducements to the committee. Inquiries from Tiffin, Xenia, and Worthington emerged, and the stage was set for the union of local boosters and religious leaders to found a college.[41] However, the inquiring communities were slow to develop an acceptable offer, while the village of Tarlton (Pickaway County, Ohio) presented an attractive bid.

The people of Tarlton, with the help of educator and Reformed Church member S. S. Rickly, quickly developed a definitive proposal of ten acres of land and subscriptions of seventy-two hundred dollars. The Synod accepted their proposal and the town's only stipulation: to name the new institution Tarlton College. However, not long after the vote of the Synod on April 18, 1850, church leaders began to question their choice and expressed renewed interest in locating the college in Tiffin. As Tarlton College began to construct its first building, church leaders dispatched an envoy to Tiffin to entice its citizens to reconsider its decision and tender a more competitive offer. This time the local boosters responded. Josiah Hedges gave the land and raised more than eleven thousand dollars to locate the college in Tiffin. Heidelberg College was born from a clear union of denominational and local booster forces.

End Notes

1   La Salle's full name was Rene Robert Cavalier Sueur de La Salle.

2   Edna Kenton, trans., *The Jesuit Relations and Allied Documents: Travels and Exploration of the Jesuit Missionaries in New France, 1610–1791* (New York: Albert and Charles Bony, 1925).

3   R. Douglas Hurt, *The Ohio Frontier: Crucible of the Old Northwest, 1720-1830* (Bloomington: Indiana University Press, 1998), 36.

4   Reginald Horseman, *War of 1812* (New York: Alfred A Knopf, 1969), 3.

5   Charles C. Huntington, *History of the Ohio Canals: Their Construction, Cost, Use and Partial Abandonment* (Columbus: The Ohio State Archaeological and Historical Society, 1905).

6   *The Northwest Ordinance of 1787.*

7   *Ohio Constitution of 1802,* Article VIII.

8   Nelson L. Bossing, *The History of Educational Legislation in Ohio from 1851 to 1925* (Columbus, Ohio: F.J. Heer, 1931).

9   Eugene H. Roseboom, *The History of the State of Ohio* (Columbus: The Ohio State Archaeological and Historical Society, 1944), 188.

10 Ibid.

11 Alexis Cope, *History of The Ohio State University* (Columbus: The Ohio State University Press, 1920).

12 Clarence H. Cramer, *Case Western Reserve: A History of the University, 1826–1976* (Boston: Little, Brown and Company, 1976).

13 Ibid.

14 John F. Stover, *American Railroads* (Chicago: University of Chicago Press, 1976).

15 Ibid., 2.

16 Ibid., 42.

17 Douglas C. North, *Growth and Welfare in the American Past* (Englewood Cliffs, N.J.: Prentice Hall, 1996).

18 Daniel J. Boorstin, *The Americas: The Democratic Experience* (New York: Random House, 1973), 120.

19 Ibid.

20 Sarah H. Gordon, *Passage to Union: How the Railroad Transformed American Life* (Chicago: Ivan R. Dee, 1996).

21 Ibid., 21.

22 George W. Williard, *The History of Heidelberg College, Including Baccalaureate Addresses and Sermons* (Cincinnati: Elm Street Press, 1897), 202.

23 Ibid., 17.

24 Bossing, *The History of Educational Legislation in Ohio,* 156.

25 Erving E. Beauregard, "Defunct Ohio Private Colleges and Universities," in *Cradles of Conscience: Ohio's Independent Colleges and Universities,* ed. James A. Hodges, James H. O'Donnell, and John W. Oliver (Kent, Ohio: Kent State University Press, 2003), 358–368.

26 Cramer, *Case Western Reserve.*

27 M. A. Leeson, *History of Seneca County, Ohio* (Chicago: Warner, Beers & Company, 1886), 79.

28 Stephen Hartzell, www.historynotebook.com.

29 Ibid, 145–146.

30 Ibid, 145–146.

31 Ibid., 145.

32 Charles N. Glaab, (1927–2009), was a professor of history at the University of Toledo from 1968 until his death in 2009. He was named professor emeritus in 2006. He authored the groundbreaking work on urban history, *History of Urban America* (New York: Macmillan, 1976). His other important works include *The American City: A Documentary History* (Homewood, Ill.: Dorsey Press, 1960); *Toledo: Gateway to the Great Lakes* (Tulsa, Okla.: Continental Heritage Press, 1982); and *Kansas City and the Railroads: Community Policy in the Growth of a Regional Metropolis* (Lawrence: The University Press of Kansas, 1993). In an article in the *Toledo Blade* on May 3, 2009, announcing Dr. Glaab's death, William O'Neal, chairman of the University of Toledo History Department said, "He was by far the outstanding urban historian in the country. His scholarship was excellent." I was honored to have Dr. Glaab as a member of my dissertation committee and an advisor to this project. Comments on Josiah Hedges and the thesis of local boosterism were a part of many communications and discussions with Professor Glaab as his student, as the Department of History's member of my dissertation committee and friend from 1999 to 2009.

33 Carl Abbot, *Boosters and Businessmen: Contributions in American Studies; No. 33* (Westport, Conn.: Greenwood Press, 1981), 1.

34 Ibid., 76.

35 Flyer of the North-western Normal School of Fostoria, Ohio, 1876.

36 John H. Strietelmeier, *Valparaiso's First Century: A Centennial History of Valparaiso University* (Valparaiso, Ind.: Valparaiso University, 1959).

37 The College was known by many names, including Ursuline College, Ursuline Academy, and College of the Ursuline Sisters. Sister Rita Mae Johns contributed to this discussion on the Ursuline Sisters' impact on education in Tiffin.

38 *Brookhovins Tiffin City Directory,* 1902–1903, 171.

39 *Wiggins Tiffin and Seneca County Directory,* 1898 and 1899; *Brookhovins Tiffin City Directory,* 1901 and 1903.

40 Acts and Proceeding of the Ohio Synod of the Reformed Church, October 4, 1849.

41 E. I. F. Williams, *Heidelberg: A Democratic, Christian College, 1850–1950* (Menasha, Wisc.: Barta Publishing Company, 1952), 27.

{Heidelberg University in 1896. The Commercial College was located in the Old Building, located to the right of the University Building.}

Chapter 3

George Williard and the Heidelberg Commercial College

The genesis of Tiffin University can be traced back as early as 1886 when Heidelberg College faculty wished to connect with a school in nearby Carey, Ohio, for the purpose of adding commercial programs to its curriculum.

Heidelberg had much success in adding the Conservatory of Music that same year and sought to replicate their semi-independent relationship with a commercial program. As with music, free space would be provided to the commercial program in exchange for teaching the academy students (secondary education), in this case, penmanship and other business-related instruction.[1]

Discussions and negotiations continued throughout the 1886–87 academic year to find a partner who could work with the college to provide commercial education. The addition of a Business College at Heidelberg received a strong boost from President George W. Williard.[2] The president lent his full endorsement to the program in June 1887. He agreed with the faculty that it would be a very attractive offering for the young people in the region and would help the college in many ways.[3] Although he repeatedly presented the faculty proposal to the Heidelberg Board of Trustees, he never received a clear direction on how to proceed. Williard even challenged the board's inability to take action, chastising them by saying:

This should not be left to the faculty, as if the board had nothing more to do than to assemble once a year to see and hear what has been done; but should take the initiative and adopt such measures as it will broaden the work and increase the influence and usefulness of the college.[4]

Nonetheless, the board's lukewarm response did not stop Williard. Devoid of any board vote, Williard and the faculty independently secured the appointment of Mr. E. W. Keen in the fall of 1888 and began business education that year. Keen established a commercial department in the college and served as its first principal. The Department of Commerce quickly enrolled students, helping Heidelberg enjoy its largest enrollment in the history of the college.[5] Attendance grew to over sixty students by the end of the second year. Williard also secured space for the new department in the first building constructed on the campus, referred to then as the Old Building and presently called Founders Hall. They shared this building with rooming students. The Old Building was built in 1851 and had recently been overshadowed by the new College Hall dedicated in 1886.[6]

George Washington Williard

George Washington Williard (1818–1900) was an effective president of Heidelberg College and was instrumental not only in transforming the college but also being credited with starting the Commercial Department that eventually became Tiffin University.

Born in Frederick, Maryland, on June 10, 1818, the future President Williard graduated from Mercersburg College in Pennsylvania in 1838, where he continued his studies in theology for an additional two years. The Eastern Synod in Greencastle, Pennsylvania, licensed

him to preach in the Reformed Church in October 1840 at the young age of twenty-two.[7] He was a well-known and respected minister, and his reputation was enhanced in the Reformed Church through his role as editor of the *Western Missionary*, the prominent publication of the church in the West. It was widely read by ministers and church members in the West, especially in Ohio.

A short, blocky man, Williard was not a typical minister or college president of the day. Religious, but not rigid, he was a respected scholar, who spoke five languages and authored several books ranging from the *Comparative Study of the Dominant Religions of the World* to two published works chronicling his time at Heidelberg College.[8] Known as a forceful speaker, he relentlessly preached sermons from Maryland to Iowa.[9]

Accomplished as he was as a scholar and a preacher, Williard's time spent as president of Heidelberg emphasized his executive capabilities, his vision, and his ability to reach beyond his religious role and build a college. His interest in starting commercial education in a collegiate environment was an outgrowth of his own business acumen. Progressive for his day, especially for a man of the cloth, Reverend Williard was a successful businessman in his own right and held a keen interest in the business affairs of the college. He personally

{George Washington Williard was president of Heidelberg College from 1866 to 1890. He was considered an outstanding college president and was a strong supporter of commercial education.}

speculated in business ventures and invested in real estate. He owned several investment properties in Tiffin and two farms in Seneca County.[10] His assumption of the presidency in 1866 began five generations of service and impact on Tiffin, Heidelberg, and Tiffin University that spanned three centuries.

From its founding in 1850 until the appointment of George Williard to the presidency in 1866, Heidelberg College struggled financially and failed to attract a large student following. During this period, few students graduated. The college claimed only forty-eight literary college graduates and seventy-six theology graduates in its first sixteen years. For most of this time, the teaching staff of the college consisted of the president, three professors, and a tutor.[11] As with most institutions, the Civil War took its toll on the college. Now the fourth president of Heidelberg, President Williard followed three weak presidencies that had failed to place the college on secure footing. Williard reflected on what he found upon his arrival in his autobiography:

When I entered upon the work of the College, I found it in a very discouraging condition with a small teaching voice and scarcely an endowment, being little more than a respectable academy. Much hard preserving labor was required to place it on solid financial basis and so improve the curriculum to make it the educational equivalent with the colleges of the land.[12]

After he had declined an offer from the Board of Trustees of Heidelberg previously, the board finally convinced Williard to accept the call to the presidency; in Williard, they had their first religious leader who keenly understood his multiple roles in building the college. Williard would add new academic disciplines, raise money, and persuade the board to progressively expand its mission.

Williard—along with his legendary financial agent, Henry "The Fisherman" Leonard—quickly began to develop the small school. Brilliantly surviving the economic downturn of 1873, Williard erased the college's debt by 1874. For the first time in its history, Heidelberg became financially solid. Williard and Leonard aggressively turned their attention to raising funds for an endowment and building a campus. Most importantly, President Williard was committed to changing the curriculum, which was narrowly focused on a classical curriculum and theological studies, by adding the practical arts. Few colleges in the nineteenth century joined this university movement as quickly and enthusiastically as Heidelberg. Adding new academic programs augmented the struggling singular nature of its literary college.

Heidelberg progressively added new academic programs. From 1888 to 1917, Heidelberg sponsored an independent business college that later became Tiffin University. During that time, Heidelberg also experimented with other innovative academic offerings such as an Oratory School, which cured speech defects, and a Department of Taxidermy, which boasted that its stuffed quails were displayed in the window of the local Wagner and Maiberger downtown drugstore.[13] During these thirty years, from time to time, Heidelberg sponsored a Conservatory of Music,

Department of Art, Department of Polytechnic, Department of Taxidermy, Graduate School, School of Oratory, School of Theology, Normal School, and most notably, the College of Business or Commercial College. These departments were in addition to Heidelberg's classical or Literary College and the Academy (secondary education), for those who were either too young or not academically prepared to enter the Literary College. By adding these distinctive departments, Williard envisioned that Heidelberg could provide offerings that would qualify them for university status. As we will later learn, a philanthropic boost helped this vision. Soon, the college administration and trustees sought to change the status of the institution from college to university, and legislation to effect that change passed in 1890. Heidelberg's new charter as a university boldly included the *new* discipline of business in the official structure of its *new* university.[14]

Entangled Relationships — Broken Loyalties

John I. Swander met his new mentor, the Reverend Williard, upon his graduation from Heidelberg College in 1859. The future president of Heidelberg College was the leading minister of the Reformed Church in the Miami Valley and served from the First Reformed Church in Dayton. Needing an assistant to serve the region's growing German-American population, Williard hired Swander, on the recommendation of then Heidelberg president Moses Kieffer, to help with church duties and edit the *Western Missionary*. Fifteen years his senior, Williard relished guidance

and training on his new protégé, both in the spiritual and in the material. Swander lived at the parsonage and quickly became a member of the family; he was well paid and was given assignments of increasing responsibility, such as baptisms and weddings. And a good minister needed a wife. Dr. and Mrs. Williard took care of that too, matchmaking and marrying the young Reverend Swander was completed during his first year in Dayton. Readied by Williard for his own church, Swander set off with his new wife for his first calling. Williard would be named the Heidelberg president six years later.[15]

Thirty years later, in 1889, John Swander, now serving a Fremont, Ohio, church, found a stranger at his door, John Kost.[16] Persuaded by his charm and enamored by his academic degrees, Swander was so taken by his new acquaintance that he invited him to stay the evening and preach at his church the next day. In Swander, Kost finally found a companion to launch his plan to secure a chancellorship in exchange for his collection of geological specimens. As secretary of the Heidelberg Board of Trustees, Swander wielded great authority, and the offer of fifty thousand dollars in natural historical objects appealed to his need to advance his name and that of Heidelberg College. Kost, a medical doctor and amateur geologist, largely developed his recent collection during his brief tenure as Florida's State Geologist.[17] Although he did effect a similar feat at Adrian College, this wasn't Kost's first attempt at shopping his cabinet and his ideas. He often tried to sell his university ideal at colleges during his long

JOHN I. SWANDER, D. D.

The Rev. John Kost, M.D.,LL. D, in whose brain this scheme for the university in Florida seems to be originated, was chosen chancellor.

Dr. Kost, though a man of varied scholastic attainments and eminent in some departments of study, has proved himself unequal to the task of gaining the confidence of the public. Almost from the outset, therefore, the University had no existence in name.[18]

In Kost's first letter of introduction to Williard, Kost describes Swander as "my true and much beloved friend."[19] In thirty years, friends come and go.

The Heidelberg University Saga

Heidelberg changed its status from a college to a university in 1890 and held that designation until 1926. Its thirty-six years as a university can be traced to a serious conflict between church leaders, board members, a sitting president, alumni, and community members that led to President Williard's resignation. A benefactor with conditions stood at the center of the conflict: the Reverend Dr. John Kost, the claimed chancellor of the University of Florida and collector of biological specimens. Kost wanted to donate his cabinet—a term used for collections of scientific and biological specimens—to Heidelberg with the condition that the college would change its status to a university and the board would erect a large building suitable to serve as a museum to house the collection. A strong-willed and somewhat manipulative board member, the Reverend Joseph I. Swander, supported Kost. Togeth-

trips between Florida and his home state of Michigan. Despite Swander's acceptance of Kost, his tenure in the chancellorship in Florida was sadly not as Reverend Kost advertised. Not known before, Kost's success in Florida was limited to securing a charter from the state. As Kost and Swander pondered a plan for Heidelberg, famed historian Herbert B. Adams completed his sixth compendium on the history of education in the states, this time Florida, and he wrote of Kost:

er, they convinced Williard and the Board of Trustees to accept the conditions. It was widely speculated that an additional condition was secretly agreed upon. In the new Heidelberg University, a new chief executive officer position of chancellor was created, and Swander promoted the naming of the newcomer Kost, a Methodist, to the position.[20]

Swander and Kost were unlikely partners in this interesting turn of events. Swander was a respected member of the Reformed Church and longtime member of the Board of Trustees. Kost was a Methodist minister, medical doctor, and professor. In the spirit of advancing the college, Swander promoted the inclusion of a museum to augment a newly suggested Polytechnic (science) Department and encouraged Kost to meet Williard to discuss the prospect of the gift of the cabinet in March of 1889.[21] Williard was initially excited about the gift, encouraged about adding Kost's collection, including such interesting artifacts as "mounted fishes, man-eating sharks, mounted birds, specimens of mammals including baboons, a sacred Himalayan monkey, six alligators, turtles, and snakes."[22] However, by June 1889, Williard and many of the trustees became skeptical of Swander's overwhelming interest in Kost and his artifacts. At the same time, Kost announced he wanted the new building to be named *The Swander Museum.*

By 1889, Williard had been president of Heidelberg College for twenty-three years. He enjoyed overwhelming support of all of the college's constituencies, and he was universally credited with rebuilding the college, erasing the debt, and building a substantial endowment for the institution. His embrace of new subjects brought the Commercial College and other innovative programs to fruition. Adding the Polytechnic Department and accepting Kost's specimens was a natural extension of his educational philosophy. He endorsed Swander's early attempt to enlarge the university through Kost's contribution and even suggested that Kost be named professor and become the leader of the newly formed Polytechnic Department. Williard investigated and later defended Kost's dismissal from the Western Michigan Methodist Conference.[23] Throughout 1889, Swander presented a series of resolutions to the Board of Trustees, many that were rushed and surprising to several of its members. He proposed resolutions to accept Kost's gifts, change the college status, erect the museum building, and of highest consequence, create the office of chancellor. Over the year, a series of highly spirited, animated, and drawn-out board meetings ensued.[24] Williard and the board members agreed, at times reluctantly, with the resolutions, and they all eventually passed. Concurrently, Swander and Williard sought and gained the approval of the Synod of the Reformed Church for the change from college to university status. All seemed well as 1890 began. That would soon change as the board sought to name a chancellor of the newly created Heidelberg University.

The Ohio secretary of state certified the new charter of Heidelberg University on March 28, 1890. Beyond the name change,[25] the revised statutes included

the establishment of a position of chancellor that

shall be the head of the university, preside at the general meetings of the faculties, and with the faculties of respective departments sign diplomas, conduct all official correspondence, and perform such other duties as are usually connected with such office. The secretary shall keep a record of joint meetings of faculties and perform such other duties as usually pertain to such office.[26]

The Commercial College (named *Business* in the charter) joined the Conservatory of Music, Art, Polytechnic, and the Literary College (and Academy) as departments of the new university. It was very clear that the chief executive officer of the university would now be the chancellor and the former title of president would represent a secondary role, if it would exist at all.

Williard was blindsided by Swander and Kost. In a meeting to approve the articles to be sent to the state of Ohio on March 18, 1890, Swander submitted a surprise motion to elect a chancellor. Williard believed it was a formality, and he would be automatically elected. Kost's name was submitted to the board along with Williard's. Kost won the election with seven votes to Williard's five. Immediately after the vote, the board

named Williard to a newly created position as president of the Literary College. Obviously affronted, Williard immediately announced his resignation effective in June 1890. A storm of controversy enveloped the college and the community. The next day, Kost tried to make amends, saying he would step aside for Williard; the board did not accept Kost's request. A few board and community members who were outraged tried to reach out to Williard and asked him to reconsider his resignation. Concurrently, organized local groups of community members and alumni challenged the board and publicly debated the university

{John Kost's infamous specimen cabinets at Heidelberg. Little did the seven Heidelberg trustees who voted for Kost over Williard for chancellor know that Kost had a long history of trading in his vast collection of biological specimens for college presidencies, honors, and favors. Kost's collegiate associations mirrored his experience at Heidelberg; they were brief, precarious, and caused severe divisions. His forty years at Adrian College were referred to as enigmatic and somewhat devious. Swander's actions eventually left him unwelcomed at Heidelberg, and he bitterly defended his support of Kost to his death.}

movement and the motives of Swander and Kost. Swander wielded great influence in the Synod of the Reformed Church and persuaded them that naming Kost was in the best interest of the church and the college. He even secured an anonymous pro-Kost editorial in the *Christian World Magazine* under the name *Justice* that was widely read and helped fuel the division. However, the many church leaders were not as easily swayed. They joined organized alumni and community groups who were relentless in their attacks on Kost, saying:

Plainly, it is the mission of these papers to show that the election of Dr. Kost as Chancellor was an act of bad faith and cannot but result in serious injury to the University and that no other name than of Dr. Williard should have been considered for the position by the board. It is the purpose of this committee to call the attention of the Ohio Synod pointedly to the subject to the end solely that the right may ultimately prevail and that the university may not suffer serious injury.[27]

Swander tried to maintain peace by reaching out to Williard. Williard decided he would not cooperate with the board any longer. His stinging letter of resignation reprimanded the board's persistent support of Kost.[28] Heidelberg lost a great president, and the Commercial College lost a great supporter.

Protests surrounded the inauguration of Kost. The board received complaints about his Methodist background, citizens said they would withhold funds from the proposed museum, and the suspicions of a backroom deal between Kost and Swander would not go away. The focus of controversy did not center as

much on the elevation of Heidelberg to a university as it did on the newfound prominence of the position of chancellor and the ouster of Williard. Dr. John Kost was inaugurated anyway on June 19, 1890. He led the new university for two years as chancellor. For the semester, Williard assumed the duties of president of the Literary College. However, in hopes of stopping the division that had developed over Kost and the university movement, the board named the Reverend John A. Peters as president of the Literary College in December 1890.[29] Kost, both a Machiavellian and an able administrator, could not undo the divisiveness he and Swander had created, and his authority as chancellor faded. He was met constantly with opposition from local alumni and community boosters even while he received undoubting support from the Board of Regents. Ultimately, the Literary College president began again to run the university. Kost resigned as chancellor in 1892, and Peters became acting chancellor. The position of chancellor quickly became secondary to the president; they were interchangeable for most of the time Heidelberg was a university. Nevertheless, for two years, Kost was clearly the chief executive officer of Heidelberg University, a fact generally lost on Heidelberg College historians.

Interestingly, losing Kost was not good for the commercial education at Heidelberg. Kost, like Williard, believed in a greater Heidelberg that included the practical arts and sciences. Williard and Kost shared the same vision for Heidelberg; albeit they did not agree who should lead as chancellor. Future leaders

{The gymnasium and museum was built in 1893 in large part to meet the proviso of John Kost's gift of geological specimens. His gift depended on the college becoming a university, creating a position of chancellor, and constructing a significant building to house his collection. In 1862, he successfully affected a similar exchange and building at Adrian College, where he received an honorary M.A. and the curatorship.

The building was also known as the Castle and the Fine Arts Building and housed the Pit, the football locker room. It was destroyed by fire on the morning of October 3, 1985.}

would be more traditional in academic vision, more religiously rigid, and more devoted to returning to the singularity of a liberal arts college. Peters, in his inauguration address in 1891, began to alter the direction of the university, making a plea to return to the classics of ancient times and condemning the university's recent trend to embrace the practical arts.[30] Peters's eleven years as president (1890–1901) were marked by financial hardship. He was burdened with the responsibility of building the new science building during a national economic depression, which resulted in a weakened fundraising atmosphere and annual operating deficits. Peters and his successor, Charles E.

Miller, questioned the efficacy of the university effort and were more comfortable in promoting the religious and classical aspects of a Heidelberg education.[31]

The university movement had a profound impact on further separating the departments Williard had founded. The Commercial College, always independent of the college, particularly distanced itself from the Literary College. Art and music, as business, operated as separate financial operations under Williard. He had hoped to bring them under the university banner during the change to university status. However, the university's emphasis on the Polytechnic Department and the board's commitment to build a museum to house Kost's artifacts overshadowed the other departments. Without Williard and Leonard, fundraising suffered, and the new building became a financial burden. Instead of bringing all of the departments together under the university banner, tight budgets left them to fend for themselves, and the separation was broadened. For the Commercial College, the collegial relationship it enjoyed under Williard became more business-like under future leaders.

Increasingly, future presidents viewed the Literary College as superior to other departments. Heidelberg viewed the art, music, oratory, academy, and commercial studies as separate divisions, each having different academic requirements and dissimilar lengths of study. Art, music, and oratory, as well as the Commercial College, were not four-year programs. In the *Aurora*,[32] the university yearbook, for example, each class in the Literary College (freshmen, sophomores, juniors, and seniors), and each division (art, music, oratory, and commercial) had their own sections. In the years before the

break with Heidelberg, the Commercial College section in the yearbook became larger and more distinctive. For all of the departments except the Literary College, independence increased dramatically under the university system. The only financial connection and obligation the independent departments or divisions had to Heidelberg University was a small per-term fee that ranged from seventy-five cents to three dollars per student.[33] The Commercial College enjoyed its independence; it controlled its own finances and governance and only looked to Heidelberg for classroom space.

{Heidelberg University in 1896. Clockwise: the Gymnasium/Museum, the Ladies Hall, the President's Residence, University Hall, and the Old Building.}

End Notes

1   Faculty Minutes of Heidelberg College, September 6, 1886.

2   Heidelberg College Board of Trustees Minutes, June 12, 1888.

3   Heidelberg College Board of Trustees Minutes, June 13, 1887.

4   Ibid.

5   E. I. F. Williams, *Heidelberg: A Democratic, Christian College, 1850–1950* (Menasha, Wisc.: Barta Publishing Company, 1952), 155.

6   Faculty Minutes of Heidelberg College, September 4, 1888, and December 12, 1888.

7   Williams, *Heidelberg*, 133.

8   George Washington Williard was a prolific writer and was very interested in chronicling the history of Heidelberg College. He was honest in his assessments of his time at Heidelberg. His works include: *Comparative Study of the Dominant Religions of the World* (Reading, Penn.: D. Miller, 1893); *The History of Heidelberg College, Including Baccalaureate Addresses and Sermons* (Cincinnati: Elm Street Press, 1897); and, *The Life, Character and Work of Henry Leonard: "The Fisherman"* (Dayton, Ohio: Reformed Publishing Company, 1890).

9   Williams, *Heidelberg*, 167.

10 Dr. N. Eugene Williard, *The Story of Three Dr. Williards of Tiffin and Seneca County*, can be found in the genealogical section of the Tiffin-Seneca County Library.

11 Williams, *Heidelberg*, 130–132.

12 George W. Williard, *The Autobiography of George Williard,* 190. This handwritten life account can be found in the Heidelberg Archives.

13 *Kilikilik*, Vol. 1 (December 1894): 66.

14 *The Charter of Amending Purpose of Heidelberg College*, which created Heidelberg University, March 28, 1890.

15 John I. Swander. *Romance in Religion: A Biographical Sketch of Dr. Swander's Life* (Tiffin, Ohio: Sacksteder Bros., 1915), 50–55.

16 Swander, *Romance*, 141–142.

17 The Florida Environmental Protection Agency website:www.dep.state. fl.us/geology. Dr. Kost was appointed by Governor E. A. Perry in 1886. The legislature terminated the position in 1887.

18 George Gary Bush, *History of Education in Florida*, No. 6, ed. Herbert B. Adams (Washington, D.C.: Bureau of Education, Government Printing Office, 1889), 47.

19 Swander, *Romance*, 150.

20 A serious and public disagreement ensued among friends of Kost and Swander (the pro-university movement/pro-Kost group) and Williard, a majority of alumni and community members (anti-university/anti-Kost group). Williard's resignation touched off an anti-university movement that was led by local boosters and concerned alumni. Detailed pamphlets were published and widely disseminated presenting each side of the case. The alumni and local boosters' case was made in the pamphlet, *A History of the University Movement*. Swander, Kost, and the Board of Regents' case were made in two pamphlets: *The Chancellorship of Heidelberg University: A Reply* and *The Chancellorship of Heidelberg University: A Reply. Part Second*. All three can be found in the Heidelberg College Archives and in their full reprints in Tiffin newspapers.

21 *A History of the University Movement*, 3.

22 Heidelberg College Board of Trustees Minutes, June 17, 1890.

23 Ibid., 12.

24 *Tiffin Weekly Tribune,* June 1890.

25 In *The Charter of Amending Purpose of Heidelberg College,* in addition to changing the name of Heidelberg College to Heidelberg University, the name of the governing body of Heidelberg College name was changed from the Board of Trustees to the Board of Regents.

26 *The Charter of Amending Purpose of Heidelberg College.*

27 *Tiffin Tribune,* September 18, 1890.

28 Heidelberg College Board of Trustees Minutes, June 18, 1890.

29 Williams, *Heidelberg,* 169.

30 John Abram Peters, *Baccalaureate and Other Addresses* (Delaware, Ohio: The Gazette, 1908), 157.

31 Williams, *Heidelberg*, 176, 217.

32 *Aurora*: A review of the Heidelberg College yearbooks from 1888 to 1917 provides an interesting view of the independence of the Commercial College and the other divisions.

33 Report of the President and Acting Chancellor of Heidelberg University, 1905.

{Commercial students pose for a class picture, 1913.}

Chapter 4

Early Leaders of the Heidelberg Commercial College

During its thirty years, the Commercial College—also called the Commercial Department, Business School, or College of Commerce at Heidelberg throughout its history at Heidelberg—operated as an independent unit while under limited control of Heidelberg's trustees and administration. The early leaders were educational businessmen who earned a living from the tuition they could collect. Heidelberg was not responsible for their salaries or their expenses. The relationship between the Commercial College and Heidelberg appears to have been defined by the necessity of the moment. For example, when Heidelberg needed the Commercial College for financial reasons, it was fully included. Similarly, when the department advertised its program, it emphasized its association with the college, and Heidelberg's facilities provided needed academic space.

At times, this rather ad hoc arrangement led to complications. However, for most of the thirty years both Heidelberg and the leaders of the Commercial College enjoyed their independence. For example, the Board of Trustees of Heidelberg College ceremonially approved the naming of the department's principal and allocated the department space on campus. Despite these administrative controls, the department was an independent financial entity. At times, when the department attempted to disassociate itself from the university or sell the property and *goodwill* of the department, the trustees tried to block such moves, only for the reason that Heidelberg should receive a percentage of the sale. On many occasions, Heidelberg showed no interest in financial transactions from principal to principal. Business students were not considered undergraduates, because the course of study was generally one year, and admissions requirements were less competitive. Enrollment was predicated by the space allocated by Heidelberg, and the enrollment dictated how much money the principal and staff of the Commercial College would earn. Understandably, the stress between the administration and the leaders of the Commercial College eventually was centered on the issue of space allocation on the Heidelberg campus. These issues and inconsistencies aggravated the relationship between Heidelberg University and the early leaders of the College of Commerce and eventually contributed to the early and rapid turnover of principals.

Early leaders of the Heidelberg Commercial College were called principals. This was common for most commercial colleges; however, what was uncommon was that a commercial college had any relationship or affiliation with a college or university. Williard's progressive view of late nineteenth-century education made this possible at Heidelberg College. With Williard gone, the Heidelberg Commercial College fate was determined by how well the principal could lead and market business education in the region. From 1892 to 1896, the trustees appointed a series of three principals who were singularly unsuccessful in making the newly named College of Commerce a financial success. During the first ten years of operation (1888–1898), four principals led the Commercial College at Heidelberg. Accomplished in the field of business education, all four struggled with space and enrollment issues on the Heidelberg campus and left to pursue more lucrative opportunities. They were followed by three longer-tenured principals, each being increasingly more successful.

E. W. Keen, the First Principal

E. W. Keen was the first principal and lead instructor of Heidelberg Commercial College. He invested his own money in purchasing equipment and furnishing the two rooms allocated to him. He led the depart-

ment for three and a half years (1888–1892). He was President Williard's choice to establish the Commercial College and develop the new program in concert with Heidelberg. Vice Principal A. G. Barone assisted Keen during this period. The Heidelberg College Catalogue for the 1889–90 academic year lists a business course of study that included bookkeeping (single and double entry), penmanship, short-hand writing and typing, and typewriting. Keen proudly promoted a classroom that was arranged as a regular business office where students "would experience the same drill they would get in actual business offices."[1]

The success of the program and the high demand for its progressive approach to business education resulted in increased enrollments and an annual request by Keen for more room on the Heidelberg campus. At its highest, the business program made up a quarter of the total enrollment at Heidelberg. Now a university, Heidelberg was slowly healing from the Kost and Williard disagreements; its new emphasis was on establishing a Polytechnic Department and building a new facility to house the department and its fallen leader Dr. John Kost. The Polytechnic Department had only ten students; the Commercial College enrollment surpassed one hundred. However, there was little interest by Heidelberg to provide more room for the Commercial College.

Keen and Barone did not mind teaching penmanship for twenty-seven Heidelberg preparatory academy students without compensation; they just wanted space to grow. Keen and Barone reported to the board that they had three recitations taking place at one time in a single classroom. At the same time, Heidelberg wanted to collect a three-dollar per-student contingent fee for each student enrolled in Keen's college. Sharing the Old Building with a dormitory did not suit Keen well. The students in the dormitory repeatedly teased Keen. His complaints to the faculty and the president received no action.[2] With little income from the Commercial College, Heidelberg showed only passing interest in allocating more room.[3]

Tensions grew between Keen, the Board of Regents, and the new acting chancellor and Literary College President John Peters over the fairness of space allocation versus student enrollment. The 110 students enrolled strained the modest space allocated to the Commercial Department and prompted Professor Keen to define the department's exact status within the institution and to seek assurances that the Commercial College's sacrifices would be rewarded in the future. During his short chancellorship, Kost tried to incorporate the Commercial Department into the university and allocate more space; the board, however, rejected his recommendations.[4] By June 1891, the Board of Regents of Heidelberg University knew that the undefined independence of departments of the newly created university was causing stress and was becoming a management problem. After the chancellorship debacle, the departments of art, business, music, and polytechnic were given more financial and management independence, while the Literary College became more centrally managed and

funded. In 1891, the board established a committee to clear the matter seeking to end any friction between departments. The committee resolved to define the relationship between the departments and the Literary College and to increase the fees of the commercial students in exchange for more room. Yet, the full Board of Regents of Heidelberg University never acted on the committee's resolution.[5] These issues remained unattended throughout the thirty years the Commercial College was housed at Heidelberg, and they remained a central issue in the future development of Tiffin University.

Unable to secure the necessary classroom space they felt was needed for growth, Keen and Barone submitted their resignations in 1892. As part of the split, they sought to personally sell the property and *goodwill* of the department to the highest bidder. However, the board refused to recognize the action and began their own search for a successor. After some deliberate negotiations, Keen and the board settled on a financial split of the assets: Keen could sell the physical assets; Heidelberg could sell the business *goodwill*.[6]

After the departure of Keen and Barone, the enrollment precipitously dropped under the next three principals (Christman, Runkle, and Replogle). Enrollment averaged in the mid-thirties throughout these five academic years. Mediocre leadership from the Heidelberg administration and the College of Commerce, lack of space, and competition from another commercial school in Tiffin—the Tiffin Business Col-

{J. A. Christman}

lege owned by Charles Clinton Kennison—all contributed to the overall stagnation of the College of Commerce from 1894 to 1898. In addition, the economic downturn of 1894 was particularly harsh on business education.[7]

J. A. Christman

The Heidelberg University Board of Regents appointed J. A. Christman to succeed Keen and Barone in 1892 as principal of the Commercial Department. He purchased the assets of the department from Keen and Barone. Christman was a graduate of Ohio Normal University's commercial department in 1889. Ohio Normal University later became Ohio Northern University in Ada, Ohio. He also graduated from Eastman National Business College in Poughkeepsie, New York. Christman came well prepared, having served at two other commercial colleges in Indiana and New Mexico. Wilda Chambers, who taught shorthand and typewriting, and was a graduate of Tri-State Business College in Toledo, assisted him.[8]

Only twenty-one students were enrolled in 1892, seven of whom enlisted for Chambers's shorthand program. Christman and Chambers's salaries came directly from tuition, and Heidelberg received a small per-student fee and three dollars for each graduating student. In an attempt to market directly against the Literary College, Christman was the first Commercial College principal to challenge the value of a liberal arts education. In the 1893 Heidelberg University Catalogue, Christman sought to increase enrollment by attracting Literary College students, saying,

Every young man and woman should obtain a thorough and practical business education. There is no comparison between the Heidelberg College of Commerce and the Commercial College of ordinary literary colleges. An investment in a Business Education will produce a larger per cent interest on the amount invested, than any other capital.[9]

This intra-university marketing sought to attract students away from choosing a literary education and was not well received by the university administration. Lack of accommodations also hurt enrollment. The regents were more interested in finding room for Kost and the Polytechnic Department.[10] Principal Christman lasted only one year. Amiable but direct, he prepared the department and the university for a transition to a new principal. As he resigned the position on May 12, 1893, he stated, "Arrangements should be made to give more room for the department, at the present, it is too compressed."[11]

{Oliver O. Runkle}

Oliver O. Runkle

The Board of Regents spent the summer of 1893 searching for Christman's replacement. They could find no one locally to take the position. Their search took them to Lisbon, Iowa, and Oliver O. Runkle became the third principal of the now-called Heidelberg College of Commerce. He boasted that he taught "actual business on the Inter-Communication Plan,"[12] and he ran the department from 1893 until 1895. During this time, his daughter, Adaline Runkle, instructed in shorthand and Viola Meyers taught English and business writing. Enrollment averaged only twenty-seven students, and Runkle could not make the College of Commerce a financial success for Heidelberg or himself. After borrowing funds from Heidelberg on a long-term note to keep the College of Commerce financially afloat, he resigned in June 1895 due to financial difficulties.[13] He eventually paid Heidelberg in full, although it took some time.

After his departure, he accepted a position at the Tiffin Savings Bank, which he held for more than twenty years. He maintained close and friendly ties with the department during that time, employing graduates and returning to campus to deliver addresses to the students from time to time.[14]

Charles M. Replogle

Rapid turnover and poor enrollment threatened the future of the Business Department at Heidelberg. Charles M. Replogle became the fourth principal of the Commercial College in 1895 and left after only two years. Only twenty-one years old when he was named principal, he was a native of Farragut, Iowa, where he graduated from high school in 1892. He graduated from Hayward Commerce Institute in 1895, after spending one year at Mount Morris College in Illinois. Young and aggressive, he brought new techniques to the Heidelberg Commercial College.[15] These included adding an ornate bank teller stand in one of the classrooms. Replogle taught the Ellis System of Actual Business Practice, which emphasized hands-on education and learning as opposed to lecture pedagogy typically offered. Confident that this would appeal to young prospective students, Principal Replogle promoted one trial week, free of charge, to students whom he believed would prefer this method to a textbook school.[16] He added an assistant, Claude H. Shumaker, in 1895. Shumaker graduated from Heidelberg University in 1893, and

{Ornate bank teller stand added to a classroom in Founders Hall by Principal Charles M. Replogle}

later from two commercial colleges: Heidelberg in 1895, and Spencerian in Cleveland in 1896. He made arrangements for commercial students to use the university's library and the gymnasium.[17]

Heidelberg liked the improvements Replogle and Shumaker made. Nevertheless, these two young men never were able to attract many students to the Commercial College. Enrollment averaged only twenty-eight students during the two years they led the school, and finances were strained. Early in his first

{Charles M. Replogle}

{Mr. and Mrs. C. C. Kennison}

year, Replogle approached the Board of Regents of Heidelberg to state that his fifteen-dollar-a-month compensation as principal could not justify him continuing.[18] He asked Heidelberg to allow him to keep all of the tuition he generated to ensure him a fifty-dollar monthly salary. Heidelberg agreed; however, as with the three who preceded him, Replogle found that he could make more money practicing the craft he was teaching. Replogle resigned to accept a position as head bookkeeper in the city gas office.[19]

Replogle's problems prompted the Board of Regents of Heidelberg University to face their inability to make the Commercial College financially self-sustaining. They considered several options: closing the college, removing it to downtown Tiffin, or supplementing it with university funds. There was little support for using any university funds; President Peters and the board pressed that all of the departments, except the Literary College, should be self-sustaining. However, the regents shared the concern of

Replogle and past principals. They wanted to afford a principal and teachers of the Commercial College "a living remuneration without using the contingent funds of the university."[20] In addition, they felt the competition from a new commercial college, Tiffin Business College, was formidable because they were located in the central business district of Tiffin. After a thorough assessment of their options in June 1896, the Board of Regents resolved that the department would exist only as a self-sustaining division and Heidelberg would purchase the "furnishings and good will of Tiffin Business College and remove the commercial department to the central part of the city."[21] This decision would have foreshadowing effects on Tiffin University.

Charles Clinton Kennison

Professor Charles C. Kennison had offered to sell his Tiffin Business College, located in downtown Tiffin, in 1895 to Heidelberg. The university first declined; however, after having three failed principalships, the administration felt they should turn to a more experienced and accomplished leader. A year later, the Board of Regents accepted the offer of Professor Kennison. At first, Heidelberg and Kennison sought to move the College of Commerce to downtown Tiffin to attract more students. Instead, the colleges were combined on Heidelberg's campus in an effort to increase enrollment. Kennison was subsequently named principal of the consolidated school on August 27, 1897, where he and the College of Commerce remained until 1903. Kennison still maintained partial ownership in the combined school and brought needed stability to the department. Kennison's wife taught stenography while Francis Blue taught bookkeeping. Initially, Kennison revitalized the school by adding faculty, starting a night and summer school, and revising the curriculum.

Kennison and the Board of Regents of Heidelberg were pleased that the terms of the new arrangement were clearly defined. Kennison assured them there would be no expense to the university whatsoever except for providing space.[22] He saved money on the merger by eliminating the rent he paid for his downtown location.[23] Kennison continued the Ellis System of Actual Business Practice begun under Replogle

Table 3.

Enrollment by Department at Heidelberg University During the Kennison Era

Department	1900-01	1901-02	1902-03	1903-04	4 Year Total	4 Year Avg.
Literary College	113	101	102	84	400	100
Commercial College	52	54	59	24	189	47
Music Conservatory	76	72	92	77	317	79
Art Department	39	40	32	50	161	40
Academy	63	53	60	73	249	62
Science	89	74	44	54	261	65
Oratory	27	43	43	30	143	36
Graduate	1	0	1	5	7	2
Theology	18	18	26	27	89	22
Pedagogy	15	9			24	6
University Headcount	493	464	459	424	1840	460
Less Counted Twice	120	123	182	107	532	133
True Headcount	373	341	277	317	1308	327
Commercial College Percent of True Enrollment	13.94%	15.84%	21.30%	7.57%		14.45%

Table 4.

Enrollment by Department at Heidelberg University During the Sterner Era

Department	1904-05	1905-06	1906-07	1907-08	1908-09	1909-10	1910-11	1911-12	9 Year Total	9 Year Avg.
Literary College	89	100	89	102	126	118	133	137	894	99
Commercial College	71	84	80	76	84	91	118	97	701	78
Music Conservatory	94	68	96	55	66	60	63	79	581	65
Art Department	34	18	58	40	43	17	30	33	273	30
Academy	70	71	58	61	62	52	59	60	493	55
Science	70	113	96	109	73	48	65	51	625	69
Oratory	37	99	26	30	40	55	51	39	377	42
Graduate	3	1	1	2	0	1	0	1	9	1
Theology	17	17	20						54	6
University Headcount	485	571	524	475	494	442	519	497	4007	445
Less Counted Twice	129	154	132	119	127	105	127	120	1013	112
True Headcount	356	417	392	356	367	337	392	377	2994	333
Commercial College Percent of True Enrollment	19.94%	20.14%	20.41%	21.35%	22.89%	27.00%	30.10%	25.73%		23.41%

and made improvements in stenography, instituting an amanuensis system of dictation.[24] Enrollment rose to a high of seventy-five students, fifty-nine full-time and fourteen part-time, once again reviving the calls for building maintenance and increased space. Heidelberg responded by adding a room vacated by the long-defunct Goethean Literary Society.

Suddenly, the stability gained was lost when a new commercial school opened in nearby Fostoria, Ohio, in 1902. The night and summer school experiment was not successful. Financial constraints were affecting both Heidelberg and the Commercial College. In an attempt to extract more income from the College of Commerce, Heidelberg renewed an old demand for a three-dollar registration fee to be paid before students could be enrolled in the business college. This strained relations between the university and the college and consequently hurt attendance of business students.[25] Enrollment in the College of Commerce remained steady through 1903; however, attendance dropped precipitously in 1904, and Principal Kennison resigned that same year.

John Foster Sterner

The university catalogue of 1903–04 included a pronouncement that "*Heidelberg Commercial College will open under the new management of John Foster Sterner, an expert accountant and with twelve* years experience as an instructor and as a principal."[26] Sterner found the Commercial College in a depleted condition upon his arrival. He would prove to be the best leader of the department to date.[27] Under Sterner, the college expanded, averaging eighty students a year during his eight years as principal (1904–1912). He, along with Waldermer Harcourt (W. H.) Howland, who served as co-principal from 1908 to 1910, reorganized the curriculum to include a more practical approach to higher accounting, bookkeeping, shorthand, and penmanship. Howland had experience in commercial colleges in Trenton, New Jersey, and Adrian, Michigan. As they raised the quality, they raised tuition. By 1908, the fifty-dollar annual tuition also entitled students of the Commercial College to take subjects taught in the Preparatory Department of Heidelberg University. Of the fifty dollars, only one dollar was passed on to Heidelberg University.[28]

The Commercial College became a financial success under the control and responsibility of Sterner, allowing it to acquire some of the best office equipment of its time in the region.[29] Sterner was the first principal to persuade the administration to significantly increase their space allocation. By 1906, the Commercial Department occupied four rooms of the Old College Building (presently Founders Hall) and, for the first time, had separate rooms for typewriting and stenography. Sterner developed eligibility rules for the Commercial College students to participate in intercollegiate athletics.[30] An interesting student in the 1911 Commercial College class was E. I. F. Williams. Williams later led the Education Department of Heidelberg College for decades and wrote a centenary institutional history of the school.[31]

The Commercial College prior to Sterner's arrival was struggling and lacked sufficient equipment and space. By increasing the quarters to four complete rooms, Principal Sterner enjoyed enrollment increases. Typewriting and shorthand occupied separately equipped rooms.

{Top: John Forest Sterner, Principal of the Heidelberg Commercial College, 1904–1912}

{Bottom: Waldermer H. Howland}

{An early marketing devise of the Commercial College: Tiffin, Ohio, postcard with John Sterner's signature}

Heidelberg University Campus.

Tiffin, Ohio.

Compliments of J. F. Sterner.

Sterner's most important contribution was to provide more adequate and up-to-date equipment than had been offered in the past. Commercial colleges varied greatly in the quality of learning tools offered. Commodious space was important to the learning experience and to the marketing of the school. Commercial colleges that depended solely on lecture and recitation often failed. In the small quarters afforded, Sterner and Howland remodeled a classroom to be identical to what students would encounter in a real business office. Students learned on calculating machines, typewriters, bookkeeping machines, and other newly created business devices. Hands-on experiences in a virtual business environment were the most attractive to students selecting his school. Sterner had intended for his students to move seamlessly between his simulated offices at the College of Commerce and their first jobs.[32]

Sterner and Howland's Commercial College was a success, and they mixed well with the Heidelberg administration. Their emphasis on quality instruction attracted students from beyond Ohio. Classes were interchangeable between the literary and commercial departments. They were the most aggressive leaders to date and marketed their school to both sexes aggressively. Their advertisements included quotes from the president of Princeton University saying, "Today the young man who graduated from the literary college and who enters business without going through a business school is enormously hampered in the progress of life,"[33] while Harriet Beecher Stowe's testimonial appealed to women: "No young lady could have better safeguard against adversities of fortune or better resources in time of need, than a good knowledge of business affairs."[34] Sterner and Howland celebrated the twentieth anniversary of the Commercial College in 1908 with an aggressive advertising campaign that promoted the merits of business education. Sterner was often heard quoting the president of the Eastman Business College saying, "A writer of shorthand who can typewrite his notes is safer from poverty than a Greek scholar."[35]

Sterner and Howland started a Telegraphy Department in 1909 to meet the needs of the railroad industry. They hired B. E. Myers as a professor of telegraphy. He had worked for the Pennsylvania Railroad and understood the daily life of a railroad operator. This railroad management program lasted from 1909 until 1911. Students mastered the daily procedures and routines of modern business, new train communication techniques, and signal work.[36]

However, Sterner had his sights on political office. In 1912, he sought a buyer of the College of Business so he could devote time and resources to run for county recorder of Seneca County, Ohio. His foray into county politics was not fruitful: Sterner, a republican, lost to democrat Louis Wagner 4,992 to 3,670 on November 5, 1912. C. L. DuPoy received 516 votes as the socialist candidate. It was a democratic year in Ohio, with the future presidential candidate James M. Cox, a Dayton newspaper publisher, winning in a landslide for the governor's seat. Sterner's political ambitions provided an interesting fate for the Heidelberg Commercial College. The next owners were to change the course of academic history in Seneca County, Ohio.[37]

Historic Purchase: F. J. Miller Becomes Principal

A loyal friendship, the political ambition of one man, an errant letter, and a fifty-mile trip all combined to bring Franklin J. Miller and Alfred M. Reichard to Tiffin to enter the enterprise of business education. In their six years at Heidelberg, they brought an educational spirit unseen by the typical denominational college. Their impact would span decades.

Franklin Miller and Alfred Reichard became associated in the summer of 1909 when Reichard became associate principal and instructor of Ottawa Business College in Ottawa, Ohio, which had been owned and operated by Miller since 1904. This meeting created the foundation of a lifetime partnership that would lead to the formation of the future Tiffin University. After two years in Ottawa, Reichard decided to pursue a master's degree.

Miller was determined to have him return to Ottawa upon completion of his degree. Noting the small population of Ottawa and the proximity of strong competing schools, Reichard began to send letters of introduction to other business colleges in the region seeking possible employment. Dr. Charles Miller, then chancellor of Heidelberg University, received one of the letters. He suggested that Reichard contact Principal Sterner directly.[38] Sterner's letter of reply made it clear that he wanted to relinquish his principalship and proffered a sale. Unable to purchase the school on his own, Reichard forwarded the letter to his friend, F. J. Miller, in Ottawa. As soon as Miller received the letter, he telegraphed Reichard to return to Ottawa so they could make the fifty-mile journey together to Tiffin. Together they met with Sterner to review the offer. Before their first visit was over, Franklin J. Miller and

Alfred M. Reichard owned the equipment and name of the Heidelberg Commercial College.

Miller paid Sterner $5,400 for the name, goodwill, and equipment of the Heidelberg Commercial College.[39] This was a hefty sum in 1912. It equates to more than $119,000[40] today. Miller gave Sterner $2,100 as a down payment and sent him $100 a month until the commitment was paid in full. The amount F. J. Miller paid to purchase the school almost shattered him financially. His continued ownership of the Ottawa Commercial College and his loan of $2,000 to his new venture for operating capital exacerbated his

Table 5.

Enrollment by Department at Heidelberg University During the Miller Era

Department	1911-12	1912-13	1913-14	1914-15	1915-16	1916-17	6 Year Total	6 Year Avg.
Literary College	137	161	192	223	236	269	1218	174
Commercial College	97	91	135	166	134	128	751	107
Music Conservatory	79	87	83	101	152	148	650	93
Art Department	33	36	41	43	30	39	222	32
Academy	60	54	54	43	38	32	281	40
Science	51	84	113	230	261	186	925	132
Oratory	39	47	59	60	53	75	333	48
Graduate	1	0	0	0	0	0	1	1
University Head count	497	560	677	866	904	877	4381	626
Less Counted Twice	120	170	193	241	219	227	1170	167
True Head count	377	390	484	625	685	650	3211	459
Commercial College Percent of True Enrollment	25.73%	23.33%	27.89%	26.56%	19.56%	19.69%		23.39%

financial circumstances. He was determined to get his investment back and more. Together, he and Reichard set out to improve the college by establishing college traditions and raising standards. Most importantly, the educational market responded.

Heidelberg had a leader in Miller much different than past principals of the Commercial College. He possessed a keen personal philosophy about the role of business education in the life of students and its role in America's progress and development. Also, he possessed a real desire to make the enterprise attractive enough to students that it would be financially rewarding for both him and Reichard. These two principles guided Miller to ensure his educational product had a successful outcome: employment. Unlike colleges and universities of the day, and other commercial colleges for that matter, Miller and Reichard did not wait for students or employers to come to them. They grew the institution on a business plan based on aggressive advertising, personalized one-on-one recruitment, and focused placement of students. This strategy, coupled with a deep and developed educational philosophy that business education deserved its rightful place at the collegiate table, proved to be a formula for success. This success eventually would force them to leave Heidelberg and strike out on their own.

With the single bicycle Reichard and Miller mutually owned, they rode trains and the interurban, placing the bicycle in the baggage car as they worked the countryside recruiting prospective students. They sat on the porches of farmhouses and around kitchen tables recruiting students and convincing parents that an investment in their school would pay long-term dividends.[41] Historically, high school graduation had been officially required for admission, but that was seldom enforced. Miller and Reichard gradually changed this stipulation, and graduation from a *first grade* high school became a requirement for matriculation. The new owners of the Heidelberg Commercial College had close competition with which to contend. Both Fostoria and Fremont, twelve and eighteen miles away respectively, had for-profit business schools. After two years of aggressive recruitment, Miller bought the Fostoria school and opened a night school there to fend off any new competitors, and the Fremont school simply closed. Miller and Reichard's hard work and entrepreneurial spirit paid off. During the five years Miller was principal and Reichard was vice principal (1912–1917), the Commercial College of Heidelberg University was never more successful. Miller and Reichard felt their institution was now on track to be a collegiate school of business of a standard university:

Now that the entrance requirement to this department of the university has been successfully established, and the enrollment has become as large as desired, the future ideal of those responsible for the success or failure of Heidelberg Commercial Department is to enlarge and strengthen the course of study until it stands upon a par with the commercial courses offered by the best institutions of America. To raise the standard and efficiency of the work performed by this department to such a plane that it no longer assumes the nature of a business college, but a Department of Commerce of a standard university, designed for the especial tasks of qualifying students for technical, executive and business administrative positions, this is our ideal.[42]

"Hippety-Klippety Hippety bang,
We're the Commercials of the H. U. Gang.
Commercials, Commercials, we're hot stuff,
Everyone knows that we're no bluff.
Re-Ri-Bi-Ji-Ki-. Commercials, Rah!"[43]

Miller Adds College Amenities

Principal F. J. Miller adopted tactics of building his department that differed from those of other academic departments at Heidelberg. Typically, the other departments were happy to remain quietly separate from the social and academic activities of the Literary College. Miller, in contrast, began adding college amenities of his own, separate but similar to those offered by Heidelberg. He was so successful in creating a college identity that the community and students viewed it as more than a department. Miller viewed these advancements as having separate college characteristics within a university structure, with an eye toward future independence. Heidelberg at first enjoyed his collegiate enthusiasm, but as time went on Heidelberg realized that these distinctions complicated the relationship and caused increased competition.

By 1913, Miler and Reichard established an official college motto, flower, colors, and a yell. The motto of the college was stated in vintage Miller style: *Practice Not Theory*. The colors were black and red, and the flower was a pink rose. The yell

proved to be a morale booster. Alumni of the Commercial College were organized separately and an annual homecoming dance was held during Christmas holiday, beginning in 1912.

Principal F. J. Miller, with the support of Coach and first Athletic Director Isaac Roy Martin of Heidelberg, organized a separate athletic program for his college and sported their own basketball team. The team was known locally as the *Heidelberg Commercials*.[44] At first, the Commercials played only in the spirited interclass series, where the Academy and the Commercials joined the Heidelberg's four classes to create a six-game season.[45] Shortly thereafter, special rules were adopted for commercial students interested in playing on the Heidelberg team and official intercollegiate play, namely "five and half hours of school room work daily, for an eight-month period."[46] A few students played on Heidelberg's varsity team from time to time, but typically the business students played on their own team. The Commercial College played competitive basketball starting in 1909, playing a mixture of college, YMCA, organized clubs, and high school teams. Miller initially offered it as a male-only sport, but quickly he recognized the attraction of fielding

{The Commercial College Basketball Teams in 1915. The three teams of the Heidelberg Commercial College: the Commercial Boys, the Commercial Girls, and the Cubans. A. M. Reichard is pictured as the faculty manager.}

women's teams. Never one to miss a marketing opportunity, Miller progressively added a women's team in 1915. Prior to the Commercial College's own women's team, local women's club teams often played before the men's contests.

Games were played throughout Northwest Ohio, and competition included teams such as the Fostoria Allens, the Krex Club of Clyde, Ohio, and the Green Springs Independents, as well as Bloomville High School, St. John High School of Toledo, and the Sophomore Class team of Heidelberg.[47] As Heidelberg, the Commercials played a few high schools. Principal Miller always accompanied his team and was known to walk through the crowd greeting the fans with an eye toward a prospective student. He particularly enjoyed returning to his hometown of Ottawa, Ohio, with his team, since it was a rarity for a proprietary commercial college to sponsor an athletic team.[48] It is interesting to note that Miller's teams participated in the interclass games even after he left the Heidelberg campus in 1917.[49]

Miller's teams were successful with their eclectic schedule, and the assorted venues often resulted in some interesting turns of events. The Commercial College basketball team was accompanied by a women's team when traveling as well as at home. Before the Commercial College organized their own women's team, they brought a local Tiffin club called the *The Cookie Girl Five,* and later its own Commercial College girls team. The two-for-one ticket and the novelty of seeing women play drew large crowds and was often

Commercial Basket Ball Team 1915-1916

E. D. Guthrie..*Manager*
Orson Smith ....*Captain*
    Vinton Dysinger ....L. F.
    Wilbur Wirt ....R. F.
    Russell Arbogast ....C.
    E. L. Guthrie......................................L. G.
    Orson Smith ....R. G.
    L. Lautermilch, E. Snyder, Wm. Kovaskitsz, Substitutes.

Record to Date

Fostoria Y. M. C. A.	12	Commercials	20
Clyde Krex Club	20	Commercials	34
Bloomville High	14	Commercials	32
Tiffin High	20	Commercials	25
Fostoria Y. M. C. A.	27	Commercials	43
Greensprings	31	Commercials	34
Defiance	31	Commercials	26

{F. J. Miller's Commercial College Basketball Team (right) and schedule (above), 1915–16. Miller used his basketball team to differentiate his school from other commercial colleges.}

featured in local newspapers. At times, the Commercials played before the Heidelberg College game, playing the Sophomore Class team. A large crowd was on hand January 21, 1915, to witness Ohio Northern defeat of Heidelberg 31–25, while the Commercials beat the Heidelberg sophomores 40–6. Sometimes, parents of an opposing high school squad objected to playing an accomplished, older player from the Commercials. To accommodate this objection, the Commercials would graciously agree to have that player sit out the second half. With the addition of students from Cuba in the Heidelberg Commercial College, Miller organized a team of their own too, and after they became

accustomed to American rules, the Cubans fielded a good team against mainly high school rivals. Basketball was beginning to be popular in Cuba, but it was not played with out-of-bound rules. The local newspaper cited that the Cuban Commercials lost a game because they could not master this new American style of basketball.[50]

The addition of an employment (in modern terms, a placement) office had the most impact on the future of the Commercial College at Heidelberg. Since 1904, records of employment were codified, and F. J. Miller took personal pride in placing his graduates in positions of trust and responsibility. Miller believed that a college could justify its existence to the community only "if it was a place where its graduates could yield the greatest service, obtain large remuneration, and secure opportunity for social and professional advancement."[51] He personally oversaw the placement of each graduate through his wide network of corporate contacts, alumni relations, and personal friendships. This program annoyed the Heidelberg administration and was in direct contrast to Chancellor Charles Miller's philosophy of religious education without the temptation of material gain.[52] Principal Miller aggressively marketed his business program, at times spending as much as a quarter of his operating budget on advertising. Most of his advertising featured the large salaries

of his successful graduates. Photographs of the graduates with headlines *Business Education Pays* appeared in every possible media outlet, including Heidelberg's student newspaper. Students longed for the day when their photographs would appear in the local newspaper announcing their new position. The advertisements would often sound this tone:

Mr. Stephens, a former Junior Orphan Home Boy, in Tiffin, has made good with a vengeance, and is already commanding $2500 per annum, Miss Griffin passed the Civil Service examination and is receiving $1500 per annum. Mr. Rosenberger is the highest salaried graduate trained by the faculty. He is the manager of the Youngstown branch office of Johns-Manville Company, and receives $6000 per annum. Miss Gladding holds an unusually responsible position with the First National Bank of Flint, Michigan, her home town, and is receiving $1600 per year.[53]

Principal F. J. Miller of the Commercial College and Chancellor Charles Miller of Heidelberg clashed over their competing philosophies about the vocational role of education. This took a public face in the form of speeches and public editorials.[54] Most were friendly debates and were designed to persuade one another. However, Chancellor Miller could never overcome Principal Miller's boldness of announcing the lucrative remuneration the commercial students were receiving.

End Notes

1   Heidelberg College Catalogue, 1889–90.

2   Faculty Minutes of Heidelberg College, February 11, 1889, and October 15, 1889.

3   Heidelberg College Board of Regents Minutes, June 19, 1891.

4   Ibid., June 18, 1890.

5   Ibid., June 17, 1891.

6   Ibid., November 7, 1892.

7   Paul Monroe, *A Cyclopedia of Education*, Vol. 2 (New York: The Macmillan Company, 1911), 144.

8   *Aurora,* 1894.

9   Heidelberg University Catalogue, 1893, 106.

10 Heidelberg University Board of Regents Minutes, June 14, 1892.

11 Heidelberg University Board of Regents Minutes, May 12, 1893.

12 *Kilikilik*, Vol. 1 (November 1894): 48.

13 Heidelberg University Board of Regents Minutes, April 2, 1901.

14 *Kilikilik*, Vol. 20 (December 17, 1913): 6.

15 *Aurora,* 1897.

16 *Kilikilik*, Vol. 2 (December 10, 1895): 85.

17 *Kilikilik*, Vol. 3 (September 1896), and Heidelberg College Board of Regents Minutes, December 1895.

18 Heidelberg University Board of Regents Minutes, November 16, 1895.

19 *Kilikilik*, Vol. 3, 131.

20 Heidelberg University Board of Regents Minutes, June 16, 1896.

21 Ibid.

22 Ibid., August 27, 1897.

23 *Wiggins Tiffin and Seneca County Directory, 1895–1896.* The Tiffin Business College was located at 107 ½ South Washington Street, Tiffin, Ohio.

24 Heidelberg University Board of Regents Minutes, June 13, 1898.

25 Heidelberg University Board of Regents Minutes, June 24, 1902.

26 Heidelberg University Catalogue, 1903.

27 *Kilikilik*, Vol. 13 (October 19, 1906).

28 *Aurora,* 1908.

29 *Aurora,* 1904.

30 *Kilikilik*, Vol. 17 (October 4, 1910).

31 *Aurora,* 1911. E. I. F. Williams's one-hundred-year history is well done. However, it ignores much discussion about the Commercial College and the separation.

32 *Kilikilik*, Vol. 13, 16.

33 Ibid., Vol. 2 (December 15, 1904): 27.

34 Ibid.

35 Ibid., Vol. 13, 16.

36 *Aurora,* 1909.

37 *The Annual Statistical Report of the Secretary of State to the Governor and the General Assembly of the State of Ohio for the Year Ending November 15, 1912, Compiled by Charles H. Graves, Secretary of State* (Springfield, Ohio: The Springfield Publishing Company, State Printers, 1913).

38 A. M. Reichard, *Reminiscing About Tiffin University,* 1957.

39 *Financial Ledger of Franklin J. Miller, Heidelberg Commercial College, 1912–1917.* F. J. Miller kept detailed records of each financial transaction in his own hand. Historians often ignore financial records or do not have access to such financial records that can provide insight. This interesting financial account illustrates the sacrifices he made to purchase the college. His personal investments in operating capital, mainly used to market the new school, are quite impressive. Miller's business knowledge is also evident in these records. He well capitalized his venture from the onset and used the money to work his recruitment plan. This is in contrast with previous principals.

40 Inflation Calculator: data.bls.gov/cgi-bin/cpicalc.pl

41 Reichard, *Reminiscing.* Miller and Reichard relentlessly recruited students. Their commitment to placing students after graduation was their best-selling point to skeptical, poor parents who view education only for the rich.

42 *Aurora,* 1916, 169.

43 *Aurora,* 1915.

44 *Tiffin Daily Tribune and Herald*, January 13, 1916.

45 *Kilikilik*. Vol. 18 (February 9, 1912): 58.

46 *Kilikilik*, Vol. 17 (October 14, 1910): 9.

47 *Kilikilik*, January 15, 1916, February 5, 1916, and December 4, 1916.

48 *Kilikilik*, Vol. 19 (February 28, 1913): 82.

49 *Kilikilik*, January 18, 1918.

50 *Tiffin Tribune,* January 15, 1916, January 23, 1915, February 15, 1916, and February 19, 1915.

51 Tiffin Business University Catalogue, 1924, 49.

52 Addresses in honor of the founders of Heidelberg College Tiffin, Ohio, delivered in Rickly Chapel by Chancellor Charles E. Miller on October 2, 1930, under the auspices of Ohio Synod of the Reformed Church and Herman Albert Klahr, *Sermons and Addresses of Charles Miller* (Fostoria, Ohio: Gray Printing Company, 1967).

53 Ibid.

54 F. J. Miller's speeches and editorials can be found in the *Aurora,* 1912–1917 (of special note: see the 1914 issue of the *Aurora*), the *Kilikilik*, and Tiffin-area papers. Chancellor Miller's speeches and editorials can be found in Ohio Synod and Reformed Church publications, the *Aurora,* and the *Kilikilik*. Each held firm views and the discussions were gentlemanly, as was the custom of the day.

Mi Buenos Desea

Chapter 5

The Cuban Experiment

Political and economic interests in Cuba brought the largest and most populous island in the Caribbean closer to the people of Tiffin, Ohio. Cuba could not have obtained its independence from Spain without the help of the United States, and the United States decided before the war was over that it wanted to establish an independent democracy, friendly to America's economic and political interests, and not a permanent territory or state. Bolstered by guaranteed U.S. military and financial protection, American capital and corporations dominated Cuba at the dawn of the twentieth century. As Cuba was the greatest sugar producer in the world and the producer of most of the sugar consumed in the United States, American capital had poured into the island during the last quarter of the nineteenth century.[1]

After Spain relinquished all rights and sovereignty over Cuba, the United States governed the country from December 10, 1889, until a U.S.–influenced constitution was adopted on February 21, 1901. America's desire for a self-governed Cuba overshadowed concern that Cuba would never really develop a tradition of democracy and tolerate political competition. Anxious to protect its economic interests in this region, as well as to secure the success of the newly constructed Panama Canal, the United States constructed military bases in the Canal Zone, Cuba, and Puerto Rico. This intense military, political, and economic involvement in Cuba at the turn of the century led to intimate connections, so close that one historian called it "as close as they can be without sharing the same flag."[2]

This close relationship between Cuba and the United States permeated every aspect of American culture, including higher education. During the first decade of the twentieth century, more students from Cuba enrolled in America's colleges and universities than from any other foreign country. From early 1914 until late 1916, the Heidelberg Commercial College under F. J. Miller and, in turn, the city of Tiffin were hosts to, and enrolled, more than one hundred students from this newly independent republic. Cubans soon accounted for a majority of students in the Commercial College and became a visible cohort in Tiffin. Heidelberg Commercial College's attraction to Cuban students was understandable. Most of them were from friendly, wealthy families with close ties to American business interests. Their parents sought to improve their status in newly independent Cuba by having an American-educated family member to advance their economic and political interests.

The Spanish-American Program

In the fall of 1914, F. J. Miller instituted a Spanish-American Department within the Commercial College at Heidelberg University specially designed for Cuban students. The initial class of forty Cuban students constituted more than a fourth of the total student body in the Commercial College. This bold move into international student markets was done with a combination of patriotic fervor and business savvy—two qualities that served F. J. Miller well throughout his life.

Miller placed Armando A. Perez in charge of his new international program. A native of Cuba and a recent graduate of Defiance College, the bilingual Perez taught English language skills and prepared the students for courses in the Commercial College. Wilfredo H. Brito, who was also from Cuba, assisted him. For young Professor Perez, this was a challenging position. He was one of nineteen seniors and the only foreign student in the small class of 1914 at Defiance.[3] Teaching English was a difficult and slow process for Perez, who was known by his Defiance classmates as more of an artist than a teacher or businessman and not accustomed to such large classes.

The infusion of foreign students, especially of one nationality, quickly influenced the culture of the campus and the community. Although the students' families were successful in commerce and politics in Cuba, both parents and students were more concerned with learning English than mastering business skills. The immersion of the Cubans in this educational setting presented more difficulties than Miller, Reichard, and Perez first imagined. Though the students mixed well on and off campus, they were much more independent than American students and were not accustomed to early twentieth-century rules of collegiate student conduct. Anxious to learn everything American, the Cuban students enjoyed and emphasized the social side of American college life. They even had their own basketball team, the *Cuban Commercials*, which played a schedule of regional high school and community teams. The popularity of the team reached Havana and was the feature story in the April 12, 1915, *La Discussion*, Havana's largest daily newspaper.[4]

At first, Heidelberg welcomed the new students (recognizing their financial potential). Soon, however, the Cuban students clashed with both the university and Commercial College administrations. Most of the disagreements centered on the lack of English language training and adequate dormitory space. Heidelberg University did not want to have such a large group of a singular nationality living together in one dormitory on their campus. Miller and Reichard continually struggled with the Heidelberg leaders for adequate space to conduct their enterprise, and the presence of forty more students, albeit Cubans, exacerbated the space problem. Eventually, Miller secured a dormitory for the Cubans halfway between the Heidelberg

ALBERT MARTIN REICHARD, B.S., M.Accts.
Assistant Principal of the Commercial Department

ZOETTA SERFASS
Instructor in Typewriting

ELIZABETH DRYFUSE
Instructor in Shorthand

WILFREDO BRITO
Assistant Instructor in Commercial Spanish

ARMANDO A. PEREZ, A.B.
Instructor in Commercial Spanish

campus and downtown Tiffin. This dormitory was the future site of the Bame Funeral Home. Nevertheless, such a large cohort of students proved hard to manage, and teaching English did not happen as quickly as all would have liked.

Armando Perez's tenure at the Commercial College was brief. After his inaugural year, Wilfredo H. Brito, his assistant, who also possessed English skills, replaced him. He was named secretary-instructor for the 1915–16 academic year. He spent that summer in Havana, successfully recruiting students and visiting his family. He soon became popular within Tiffin social circles and offered Spanish language lessons to the community at 21 Court Street in the evening.[5]

The Tiffin Community Response

Although never really accepted by the leaders of Heidelberg University, the Cuban students were well received by the people of Tiffin. The students were very popular with the citizens and boarded with some of the most prominent members of the Tiffin civic leadership. The mayor and the leaders of the chamber of commerce were particularly interested in their welfare and encouraged their stay in town. Cuban-American relations were important to the economic interests of the nation, and local business leaders sought to strengthen their own economic interests with Cuba and relished the opportunity to mix with the Cuban students. The Cuban students spent lavishly and thus were welcomed at local retail establishments. The students and civic leaders organized many jointly

{Far left: Built in 1904, the Shawhan Hotel was considered one of Ohio's finest hotels. Its Emerald Room was the home of elegant parties and celebrations. Photo courtesy Arthur Graham and Rochard Focht.}

{Left: Wilfredo H. Brito led the Cuban program through ups and downs.}

sponsored events, including Spanish lessons for local residents, cooking demonstrations, elaborate banquets celebrating Cuban independence, and military parades honoring Spanish-American War veterans. It would prove to be the most interaction local business boosters had with the college in some time.

On May 20, 1915, on the occasion of the thirteenth anniversary of Cuba's independence, the city and the Cuban students joined together to celebrate the occasion and to honor the military heroes of the Spanish-American War. Smells of essence of fowl, roasted squab chicken, and candied sweet potatoes, combined with Cuban cigars, filled the Shawhan Hotel as forty of the country's most prominent military leaders were introduced as guests of honor. This occasion marked the first time that Tiffin celebrated the independence

of a foreign country, and it showed the real affection that was mutually shared between visitors and city fathers. With the mayor serving as toastmaster, toasts went well into the night lauding the strong commercial relationship between the two countries. The coverage of civic and local leaders in Tiffin observing the day of independence headlined the local paper.

Tiffin's civic leaders continued to express fondness for the Cuban students of Heidelberg Commercial College, sometimes to the point of excess. They monitored the welfare of the Cuban students with intense closeness, and their health was of particular interest and frequently reported in the local paper. Cuban stu-

ROY

RUNS THE

EMPIRE

Always the Best

Meal Tickets

Twenty-one Meals

— for —

Four Dollars

{The Empire Hotel was just south of the Remmele Building at 160–164 South Washington Street. As the Empire, and later the Gibson Hotel, they catered to Tiffin University students for more than fifty years.}

dents mixed with locals at the Empire Restaurant at 162 South Washington Street. The Empire Restaurant was part of a large hotel owned by Charles Geyer. Its billiard hall, barbershop, and restaurant were popular gathering places for Tiffinites, American and Cuban alike.[6] On more than one occasion, the Empire was the scene of a student malady. When Felix Cabera fainted on Washington Street just after finishing supper at the Empire, a large crowd gathered to attend to his welfare. The *Tiffin Daily Tribune* reported daily on his condition, ending with news that he only had a bad case of indigestion.[7] Moreover, when Angel Consuianagia "suffered a slight stroke of paralysis as he was eating breakfast at the Empire,"[8] locals attended to him after he fell from his chair and was not able to assist himself. Civic leaders took the same care for Paul D'Scott, shielding him from the news that his father, a wealthy Havana banker, had committed suicide. D'Scott finally learned of his father's death two weeks later when he met his mother in New York City where she told him the news personally.[9]

Miller and Reichard enjoyed the newfound success of their Heidelberg Commercial College. Their school was popular within the Tiffin community and among prospective students. On March 26, 1915, the registrar of Heidelberg University announced that the enrollment of the university had increased by 65 percent.[10] Miller and Reichard took great pride in this announcement knowing that the record 164 students enrolled in their college, due in part to the large numbers of Cubans, constituted more than one-fourth of the total enrollment of Heidelberg.

As in the past, enrollment successes with the Commercial College forced Miller and Reichard to request more space from Heidelberg. With the community taking an active interest in the affairs of the commercial school and the financial impact evident on both Heidelberg and its town, Miller thought that Heidelberg would view his renewed request with more favor. However, Heidelberg Chancellor Charles Miller and the Board of Regents continued their lack of interest and aloofness toward the Commercial College and refused to allocate additional space.

F. J. Miller's discontent with the Heidelberg administration over inadequate housing and academic space became more and more public. Miller announced in early 1915 that unless Heidelberg would respond positively to his requests, he would have to discontinue the Spanish-American program at the end of the academic year. Reaction to this threat prompted quick responses by both the Cuban students and the community. For the Cuban students, the majority holding more of a predilection to learn English than business, seized this as an opportunity to enter the Academy, the preparatory school of Heidelberg University, to continue their studies. They presented the faculty with a petition to this effect, asking to have their wishes codified in a contract. After some consideration, the faculty rejected their request for a contractual relationship. However, they allowed the students to enter on the same basis as other students. At the same time, the Tiffin community sought to save the Cuban program.

The fate of the program warranted almost daily monitoring by the local chamber of commerce. The directors of the chamber instructed their executive secretary to communicate directly to them between monthly meetings via a series of letters to ensure that all was being done to keep the Cubans in Tiffin. In an open letter to the people of Tiffin in the local paper, Executive Secretary Sutherland shared the sentiments of the chamber:

Here is a matter on which I shall appreciate if you can give me your prompt advise, I understand that some half dozen Cuban students at Heidelberg contemplate leaving Tiffin within a very short time, saying that there they do not get sufficient training in English speaking. We are inadequate if we let them leave. Our business is to bring people to Tiffin and keep them here. These boys come from the best families in Cuba and spend a great deal of money in Tiffin. Many cities are spending thousands of dollars to get community publicity in Spanish speaking countries. In this city you have thirty-two publicity agents writing about Tiffin to the best possible connection in Spanish speaking countries. America has to-day the greatest commercial opportunities of its history. One of the requirements is the knowledge of Spanish. If Tiffin is alive to her opportunities, she will make an opportunity to get knowledge of Spanish in return for what these boys want. Let's not go to sleep on the job.[11]

All of this activity led to a constriction of the Spanish-American program in the Commercial College at Heidelberg. The Cuban students were now scattered among different programs: Some entered the Academy, a few became freshmen in Heidelberg's traditional undergraduate college, and eight students continued in the commercial program now under W. H. Brito, who had replaced Perez.

Echoes From Heidelberg's Cuban Department

Actual sentences written by the Cubans in their English work.

1. I never saw nobidy smother but I saw a man a boy suffocated.
2. I went to store shoe and show some some shoe and I bought a pear.
3. In Christmas we went to skate the park.
4. I commence a office and did not the finish.
5. The birds making their home of straw and others the making of branches and leaves and mud by into.

1. The last days it was here much cold and all the people was shiver because we had not gas by the stove.
2. I saw in a picture show, two train in a shock and it was terrible.

1. The men that have good heart like give shelter to the poor people. These men are reward for God after that they dead.
2. The last days I shiver a few because that I was very cold.
3. In our class always has silence and the Professor never have to knock the bell.
4. When the locomotives shock, always die the persons that go in the first carriage.
5. I think to ship very soon for Cuba and there to work, for I desire to have money.

The Beginning of the End

By the beginning of the 1915–16 academic year, Miller and Reichard recognized the difficulties in running such a program. Reichard, who just a year before had welcomed the Cubans with one of his elaborate pen art sketches of two swans over the words *Mi Buenos Desea* (My Dear Friends), now used words like *to our sorrow* and *a million headaches* to describe the program. He particularly disliked that some students were not applying themselves.[12] F. J. Miller advocated a smaller program. Finally, with more American students interested in attending and little room still available; Miller and Reichard considered retrenching the program.

Brito struggled to maintain the smaller, yet substantial Spanish-American Department. He spent some of the summer of 1915 in Havana recruiting students and promoting the college. He returned with seventeen Cubans, among them his sister and three other women, who after a short visit in Tiffin, went on to a girls' school in New Lexington, Ohio. When classes began in September 1915, the Commercial College announced its largest enrollment to date. The almost two hundred students, which included twenty Cubans, pushed the Heidelberg facilities to the limit.[13] However, this smaller class of Cubans did not mean a quieter one. As Miller and Reichard raised the admission requirements, they also asked the Cuban students to be more responsible, both on and off campus. The independent Cubans did not respond well to such an academically focused experience.

The path to more academic rigor and decorum on the part of the Cubans took a strange turn during the ensuing year—to the Tiffin courthouse. A few Cubans turned to physical assaults to retaliate for perceived injustices. Gustavo Grua was fined twenty-five dollars and court costs for assaulting Principal and Professor Franklin J. Miller on August 2, 1916. According to court records, Grua admitted that he assaulted Miller and tried to justify it on the grounds that he had been insulted by a letter from Miller stating his expulsion from the Commercial College. Even more shocking was that Wilfredo H. Brito, Miller's own choice to lead the department, was also charged with threatening Miller and bound over to the Court of Common Pleas along with Grau.[14] Brito went on to start his own school—named Tiffin Business College—for the Cubans and others upon his release from jail until Constable Graveldinger closed it on December 29, 1916, after only four months of operation. Having three Cuban students, Brito's school was an academic and financial failure. It was stopped after several writs of attachment, amounting to a considerable sum, were not paid.[15] After two years, the grand Cuban experiment of the Heidelberg Commercial College came to an end.

End Notes

1 Glenford D. Howe, *Higher Education in the Caribbean: Past, Present, and Future Directions* (Kingston, Jamaica: University of the West Indies Press, 2000).

2 Ibid., 10.

3 *Oraculum,* Defiance College Yearbook, 1914.

4 *Tiffin Daily Tribune and Herald,* Evening Edition, September 19, 1915.

5 *Tiffin Daily Tribune and Herald,* September 20, 1915.

6 *Polk City Directory,* 1892–93.

7 *Tiffin Daily Tribune and Herald,* January 11, 1915.

8 *Tiffin Daily Tribune and Herald,* May 8, 1915.

9 *Tiffin Daily Tribune and Herald,* Evening Edition, March 15, 1915.

10 *Tiffin Daily Tribune and Herald,* March 26, 1915.

11 *Tiffin Daily Tribune and Herald,* January 1915.

12 A. M. Reichard, *Reminiscing About Tiffin University,* 1957.

13 *Tiffin Daily Tribune and Herald,* September 24, 1915.

14 *Tiffin Daily Tribune and Herald,* August 3, 1916.

15 *Tiffin Daily Tribune and Herald,* December 30, 1916.

{Nine Cuban students pose in 1915.}

Chapter 6

Liberal Versus the
Practical Returns

Chancellor Charles E. Miller of Heidelberg was faced with the same dilemma that most denominational colleges and universities struggled with for most of the early twentieth century: how to balance learning with piety.[1] Expanding subdivisions of knowledge, the elective system, the establishment of land grant colleges, and a growing interest in college as a place to achieve one's vocational ambitions were threatening the denominational colleges and made it difficult for Heidelberg to be both a diverse university and focused on religion.

Miller was admittedly more comfortable combining learning with faith and was antithetical to the practical arts, especially business.[2] He held a professorship at the Heidelberg Theological Seminary at the time of his election to the presidency and chancellorship of Heidelberg. Well accepted by the Board of Regents and the community, he quickly surprised both by stating that endowment building, financial affairs, and increased enrollment would not be his highest priorities. He felt that by emphasizing the religious nature of the institution Heidelberg would prosper in the long run.

Many Ohio colleges also embraced the university movement along with Heidelberg. From 1910 through 1926, many institutions that became universities returned to collegiate status, citing that the singularity of a college clarified its educational purpose as a Christian arts college. As quickly as Heidelberg embraced the university movement, the school followed the trend to moved back toward being a Christian liberal arts college, centered on the classics, religion, literature, and philosophy. Chancellor Miller believed that the university movement at Heidelberg was a mistake as well, and he felt his energies were being spread over too disparate of an academic area. Most of Charles Miller's long and distinguished presidency and chancellorship (1902–1937) at Heidelberg was characterized by opposing the university movement and supporting a much more focused and religious college.[3] With the expanding public high school system, Heidelberg, like other church colleges, closed their preparatory academy in 1917 without much regret.[4] The summer school was also discontinued. Over time, Chancellor Miller smartly accepted the normal curriculum and music and art education and officially incorporated them under the auspices of Heidelberg. However, many of the academic experiments to grow Heidelberg were eventually discarded. Chancellor

Miller's constriction was at odds with the contemporary educational terrain; Warren Nord describes the landscape prior to Miller's leadership at Heidelberg.

Classical education was clearly living on borrowed time, and its decline was swift

in the second half of the century. It was, after all, largely incompatible with the spirit of the country: egalitarian, individualistic, experimental, practical committed to liberty and progress. High schools began to proliferate at the end of the nineteenth century under pressure of vocationalism and utility. The classical curriculum maintained a toehold in colleges only if it could keep some distance from public pressures, by the end of the century it was clear that science, vocationalism utility, pure research pragmatism, specialization, and the elective system had united to dethrone the classical curriculum.[5]

Chancellor Miller and Principal Miller's public debate became more public as Principal F. J. Miller marketed his practical education philosophy directly against the liberal arts curriculum, announcing:

Practically every college, every technical school, and even the correspondence school makes their appeal today upon a commercial basis, that is, the greater earning power and rapidity of promotion for their graduates. Colleges are pointing to their graduates who are holding positions in the professions, and State and Government offices. The technical school points to graduates who are holding responsible positions of trust and profit. This does not mean that these schools unduly emphasize the desirability of acquiring large sums of money, but it does mean that each recognizes that money in certain quantities is more or less essential to the happiness of each individual, because of the material necessities and comforts of life which it provides.

There is also recognition today that a training which will actually enable a person to do things of value is just as highly cultural as those which lead to theorizing and ministering to the aesthetic tastes. The Commercial Department of Heidelberg believes that it is tendering a far more beneficial and lasting service in behalf of its graduates by qualifying them to command a high compensation than by developing their aesthetic natures, and leaving them without the ability to gratify that nature. It further believes most emphatically that theorizing and philosophizing by educational institutions is rapidly becoming a matter of history.[6]

It became clear that the two competing philosophies could not exist under one academic roof. Chancellor Miller's predilection toward constricting the offerings at Heidelberg and Principal Miller's interest in growing the commercial program were clearly at odds. Throughout the 1915–16 academic year, tensions heightened between the two Millers, leading to a parting of the ways.

The Breakup

Enrollment grew from 91 in the first year of F. J. Miller's leadership to a high of 166 by 1917. This growth was supported, in part, by the addition of a Spanish-American Department. F. J. Miller created a successful college that held its own distinctive character. Miller's aggressiveness in promoting the College of Commerce originally pleased the Board of Regents; however, as time went on its independent success caused friction. He took rightful delight in the increased enrollments and improved student quality, as he continued to push for recognition of the importance of commercial education. The Heidelberg Commercial College was at capacity and could not grow without more space allocation from Heidelberg. During the 1915–16 academic year, Principal Miller and A. M. Reichard requested more space from Heidelberg so they could increase enrollment to two hundred students. Concurrently, Chancellor Miller became active in the Young Men's Christian Association (YMCA) movement and sought to increase their presence on the Heidelberg campus. He was more interested in providing room for the YMCA than increasing the space for F. J. Miller's Commercial College, which already occupied six rooms in the Old Building. This aggravated Miller and Reichard. As talk circulated that Heidelberg wanted to displace the Commercial College with the YMCA, Miller and Reichard prepared for the inevitable. They rented a second-floor downtown office space at 21 ½ Court Street and began offering overflow courses at this downtown location as a temporary solution.[7] Without more space, Principal Miller feared expansion was impossible. However, Miller and Reichard were looking forward; they had been considering for some time founding a business school that mirrored the newly popular junior college of the day. Although years of planning and research were in place, the thoughts of securing a new location and the necessary equipment dissuaded them. They needed time to find the right location that would ensure growth and rationalize the move.

By early 1916, it was clear that Principal Miller could not overcome—even with his charisma, success, and progressive educational approach—what

{Rev. Dr. Charles E. Miller, longest-serving president of Heidelberg, 1902–1937. Enrollment precipitously dropped (650 to 331; 51 percent) at Heidelberg after the Commercial College left. Miller used this opportunity to refocus the institution to its classical and religious roots and return to college status. His increase of religion requirements and his strict social conduct rules forced students to rebel, once destroying the front porch of the president's home. He reluctantly allow card playing and dancing, although he vowed to never attend these activities.}

others before him tried and failed to do. Chancellor Charles Miller and the Board of Regents of Heidelberg University rejected Miller and Reichard's request for more space to increase enrollment in June 1916. At that same meeting, F. J. Miller was admonished for establishing the Spanish-American Department and the regents made it clear that

all announcements of the Spanish American Department in Heidelberg University was unauthorized and disapproved by the Board of Regents and that the said principal is requested to confine his work in the Commercial Department absolutely to the usual commercial subjects.[8]

Moreover, Chancellor Charles Miller and Principal F. J. Miller's philosophical differences on the role and method of education in the early twentieth century could not be bridged. At the June 1916 meeting of the Board of Regents, the regents voted to discontinue the Commercial Department at the end of the 1916–17 academic year. The shortage of academic space on campus, the addition of the Cuban students, the emphasis on lucrative job placements after graduation, and the lack of interest of Heidelberg to really embrace the university movement exacerbated relations between the two organizations. Nonetheless, it appears the real reason for the breakup was the dichotomous philosophies of the two Millers, summed up in Chancellor Miller's report to the Ohio Synod of the Reformed Church.

For twenty-eight years, this institution has maintained a Commercial Department. It has always been financially independent of the University. Although never more prosperous than during the last five years, we believe the time has come to discontinue this Department. Its courses cover a short period of time and the big appeal to the student is chiefly financial reward. All this is contrary to the spirit and purpose of Heidelberg, and hinders us in our great work.[9]

Chancellor Miller realized his wish for a smaller Heidelberg. The total university enrollment dropped 50 percent the year after the Commercial College moved to its new campus. With the absence of the Commercial College and the other constrictions of the academic programs, Heidelberg became a much different place than the one envisioned by President Williard.

Principal Miller accepted Heidelberg's decision, although he wanted more time to effect the move. A building needed to be secured and architects needed to be hired. Miller wanted the new building to have an educational impact with space enough for expansion. In late 1916, he hired Lima, Ohio, educational architects of McLaughlin and Hulsken to redesign a downtown building. He asked the regents to allow him to continue throughout the 1917–18 academic year, but the board refused his request.[10] Principal Miller stubbornly ignored the board. He did not vacate the rooms in the Old Building and continued to advertise as the Heidelberg College of Commerce in the local paper to dispel assertions by Heidelberg that he was discontinuing the Commercial College. The conflict became heated, and threats of lawsuits were made on both sides. Since ownership of the Commercial College resided with F. J. Miller, Heidelberg finally agreed to negotiate. Principal Miller emphasized that negotiations should center on his ability to secure the proper location so he could expand and that Heidelberg should refrain from any actions to hinder him. They agreed that Miller could stay until his new downtown building was remodeled.[11]

Miller and Reichard felt the time was opportune to embark on moving the Commercial College away from Heidelberg's aegis and establish a renewed institution devoted to raising the standard of business education. Just before Christmas in 1917, in the dawn of its thirtieth year, F. J. Miller and A. M. Reichard's Commercial College finished its last semester on the Heidelberg campus.

Table 6.
A Enrollment Comparison before and after the Commercial College left Heidelberg University, 1916–1917 and 1917–1918.

Department	1916–17	1917–18
Literary College	269	263
Commercial College	128	
Music Conservatory	148	97
Art Department	39	18
Academy	32	
Science	186	70
Oratory	75	
Graduate		
University Headcount	877	448
Less Counted Twice	227	117
True Headcount	650	331
Commercial College Percent of True Enrollment	19.69%	

End Notes

1   Sherman B. Barnes, "Learning and Piety in Ohio Colleges, 1900–1930," *The Ohio Historical Quarterly* 69, no. 4 (1960): 214–243.

2   Chancellor Miller's public sermons and addresses during his Heidelberg presidency were staunchly religious and entrenched him firmly in the classical literary college camp. He, as E. I. F. Williams says on page 203 of his well-done institutional history, "bewails the godlessness of the colleges and expressed his nostalgia for the good old days when student were truly religious and had not yet been afflicted with modern heresies." His addresses can be found in the Heidelberg Library. See addresses in honor of the founders of Heidelberg College, Tiffin, Ohio: Delivered in Rickly Chapel by Chancellor Charles E. Miller on October 2, 1930, under the auspices of Ohio Synod of the Reformed Church and Herman Albert Klahr, *Sermons and Addresses of Charles Miller* (Fostoria, Ohio: Gray Printing Company, 1967).

3   Sherman B. Barnes, "Learning and Piety in Ohio Colleges, 1900–1930," *The Ohio Historical Quarterly* 69, no. 4 (1960): 214–243.

4   E. I. F. Williams, *Heidelberg: A Democratic, Christian College, 1850–1950* (Menasha, Wisc.: Barta Publishing Company, 1952), 176, 215.

5   Warren A. Nord, *Religion and American Education: Rethinking a National Dilemma* (Chapel Hill: The University of North Carolina Press, 1995).

6   *Aurora*, 1915, 152.

7   *Lawrence and Company Directory of Tiffin*, Vol. 2 (1915): 68.

8   Heidelberg University Board of Regents Minutes, June 16, 1916.

9   *Acts and Proceeding of the Ohio Synod of the Reformed Church*, October 5, 1918, 28.

10 *Tiffin Daily Tribune and Herald*, June 13, 1917.

11 *Tiffin Daily Tribune and Herald*, September 25, 1917, and October 18, 1917.

Chapter 7

Tiffin Business University
(1917–1939)

On Friday, January 14, 1918, the Heidelberg Commercial College officially closed. Approximately eighty students from Heidelberg transferred to start classes four days later on Tuesday, January 18, 1918, at the new Tiffin Business University. Franklin J. Miller rented four rooms on the third floor of one of downtown Tiffin's largest and most modern buildings, the Remmele Building. He managed the change in location with only one day of classes lost. On December 10, 1917, with a ten thousand-dollar personal investment by F. J. Miller, Tiffin Business University began operating as an incorporated institution.

With the ten thousand-dollar stake, Miller equipped the Remmele Building with the finest equipment available to accommodate more than two hundred students. New courses of study were adopted; new faculty were added; and a new catalogue was developed featuring higher accounting and management. The typical one-year courses were dropped in favor of two-year courses, which was a progressive departure.

With a paternal fervor and an entrepreneurial flair, President F. J. Miller set out to build Tiffin Business University into the quintessential business college of the twentieth century. The 1920s were a time for physical, academic, and enrollment growth, both for American higher education and Tiffin University. Miller, together with his partner and co-founder Alfred Reichard, was determined that their students would not only have the best facilities possible but also the strongest possible academic program. The move to the Remmele Building proved to be beneficial for the newly reorganized institution. The new facilities were a source of pride. The new catalog featured pictures and descriptions boasting that the facilities were *modern to the minute*.[1] At last, Miller and Reichard were not constricted by space, and the founders now turned their sights toward advancing the academic stature of the university.

Founders of Tiffin Business University

The story of Tiffin University's first half-century is largely the story of two remarkable men, Franklin J. Miller and Alfred M. Reichard. The two very different men complemented each other well. Miller was a gregarious educational entrepreneur, and Reichard was the gentle academic. Educational collaborators since 1909, they met at the Ottawa Business College, purchased and built the Heidelberg Commercial College together, and then founded Tiffin Business University, serving together for more than forty years.

{Left: Franklin J. Miller}

{Right: Alfred M. Reichard}

Miller described their friendship as close as Damon and Pythias.[2]

Together, they chose the name Tiffin Business University—often referred to affectionately as TBU—for their new school.[3] As was popular in the day, they chose a business-like name, indicating location and function of the school. Reichard insisted on including the word *university*. He admitted it showed some brashness and could be misleading. However, they wanted to signify to all who would listen that they possessed a commitment to raising the academic standards of the school. Adhering to the lofty title, they quietly contemplated the gradual and orderly development of a full-scale university, which would carry on under a self-perpetuating board after their deaths.

Franklin J. Miller

Franklin Miller was born in Garrett, Indiana, in 1880. He was only a few months old when his father, an engineer for the Baltimore and Ohio Railroad, was killed in a railroad accident. After the accident, he and his mother moved back to live with her parents in Putnam County, Ohio. They lived there until 1892 when she married John Ewing, a Hancock County farmer. Miller enjoyed a good relationship with his stepfather and stepbrother, Guy Ewing, who would later join him in the commercial education business in Tiffin. As a child, Miller worked on the farm for fifty cents a day. He was a hard worker and credited his strong work ethic to his farmhand experience and his close relationship with his stepfather. After attending a variety of common schools throughout Hancock and Putnam counties, he finished high school at McComb High School and then graduated from the now-defunct Crawfis Normal College in 1900. Following the familiar pattern of the day for promising young men—and fulfilling his mother's wishes—he entered the teaching field in a little red schoolhouse in rural Putnam County, spending his summers attending college. From his modest teaching salary and from his work on the farm, he managed to save enough to attend Tri-State College in Angola, Indiana, for a semester and later completed the year of commercial training at Lima Business College in Lima, Ohio.

After teaching for three years, Miller wanted to secure an industrial position to improve his future. His annual teaching salary of $240 was "too low to allow him to participate in life's most desirable attainments, including the maintenance of a home, much less the purchase of a home."[4] During his time at the Lima Business College, he worked after school and on Saturdays to learn the commercial college business and served as a stenographer in the Lima courts. One of his jobs was to field and answer requests for placements of students from employers. He took particular interest in a request for principalship of the Ottawa Business College in Ottawa, Ohio, that was not far from his home. He applied immediately, securing the position and doubling his former salary.

At age twenty-two, Miller was managing the struggling business college in the small town of Ottawa, Ohio. He developed a winning formula for success in this small school that would serve him well: aggressive advertising, quality instruction, and an unrelenting job placement of graduates. He quickly doubled, then tripled, the enrollment. Ottawa Business College was an educational and financial success.

Such large attendance necessitated the need for an assistant principal at the school. Although Miller made a number of friends and business associates at Ottawa who would later help in Tiffin, no friendship was more important or significant than his relationship with A. M. Reichard. Their lifelong association led them to buy the Heidelberg Commercial College and found Tiffin University. In the summer of 1909, Reichard became the associate principal and an instructor at Ottawa Business College. Reichard spent two years with Miller in Ottawa, and the two men became close friends. By making the Ottawa Business College a profitable school, Miller earned enough to save money to purchase the Heidelberg Commercial College in 1912.

Miller received advanced commercial training in Washington, D.C., at the National Commercial Institute and received an L.L.B. degree in law from the American Law University of Los Angeles, California. He married his wife, Belvia (Belle), on June 16, 1904, and together they adopted two war orphans whose mother was deceased and whose father was a soldier in France.

F. J. Miller was caught up in the spirit of educational reform and wanted to possess his own educational institution to serve people who wanted to improve their personal situation. He believed in the still-vigorous Protestant work ethic and generally promoted a philosophy that Godliness can have material rewards. He considered himself a self-made man and enjoyed the stories of Horatio Alger about serious-minded, hardworking young men who overcame their limitations and made millions. Miller knew that the for-profit educational enterprise was a peculiarly American institution, one that could hold the keys to the American Dream of its citizens. Privately owned and managed, it was an educational business that was, like other businesses, dependent on its customers. Miller quantified customer satisfaction in his enterprises on the ability of his graduates to secure employment. He ensured that his customers had a job when they graduated, which became a hallmark of his educational philosophy that he perfected throughout his life.

Miller held outside business interests in industry and was active in educational, community, and religious work. He was secretary-treasurer of the Vega Separator Company and served as a director of the Columbus Mutual Life Company in Columbus. He was president of the Seneca County Sunday School Association and a member of the Board of Reference of the Ohio Children's Home Society. Often, he was called upon in Tiffin to take community leadership

{TBU Faculty and Coaching Staff, 1928: Front row, left to right: Coach Marjorie De Ran, Hazel Stine, and Adella Shedenhelm. Middle Row: F. J. Miller, Coach Ralph Gust, Carlton Stickney and E. M. Huth. Back Row: C. L. McKillip, and A. M. Reichard.}

roles and was a prolific speaker and orator. He ran for the Ohio state legislature twice.

Miller was a rigid man of temperance. Following the passage of the resolution submitting to the states the National Prohibition Amendment to the Constitution of the United States by the U.S. Senate on August 1, 1917, and the House of Representatives on December 18, 1917, Miller founded the Seneca County Dry Federation.[5] He publicly tangled with the local Liquor Dealers Association in his role as campaign manager for the organization and sought to influence the upcoming state representative's race for Seneca County.[6] He began working with the Democratic, Republican, and Prohibition parties to stack the primary ballots with "bone-dry men." Meeting vigorously with the parties, he sought to place more than one dry candidate on each party's primary nominating ballot. He even agreed to run as a dry candidate on the Republican ticket, hoping all nominees would be dry and he would not have to campaign, since he was only concerned with electing a representative who would go to Columbus and vote for the proposed Eighteenth Amendment. His plan backfired. A single wet candidate beat Miller's two self-selected dry candidates in the Democratic primary. The split of the dry vote in the Democratic primary left Miller as the only dry candidate on the general election ballot in November.[7] He became a reluctant candidate.

Miller was in a tough race. After the August 13, 1918, primary, he stood alone as the sole dry candidate for a seat as the state representative. At that time, there was one state representative elected for each county. However, Ohio only leaned slightly against the prohibition issue, and the city of Tiffin tended to support home rule and had a powerful election block in countywide elections.[8] Miller's off-and-on campaign and reliance on one issue did not serve him well in the general election. He described himself as an unintentional candidate in this advertisement:

Professor Miller is an accidental candidate, and certainly not an aspiring candidate. His acceptance of the nomination and election would mean a heavy sacrifice upon his part. As President of Tiffin Business University and part of the teaching faculty, he has attendance of one hundred in his classes. He is the Secretary-Treasurer of Vega Separator Company and is a director of the Columbus Mutual Life Insurance Company. The salary of $1000 per annum, the amount paid to State Representatives, is very insignificant compared to his present business associations. Any method whereby a dry representative could be sent from Seneca County to the next session of the Ohio General Assembly was his aim and purpose. Professor Miller was induced to accept this nomination to assist in bringing about a nationwide prohibition by ratification of the Federal Dry Amendment by the Ohio Legislature.[9]

The vote was closer than many predicted. Miller lost by only 112 votes out of 8,948 cast. He received 4,339 votes, and his Democratic challenger F. A. Hinchey tallied 4,451 votes. The Socialist candidate, William M. Ralston, received 158 votes.[10] Seneca County sent a wet candidate to Columbus. However, Miller and the Seneca County Dry Federation prevailed in the end. The Ohio General Assembly ratified the Eighteenth Amendment to the Constitution in early 1919, and it went into effect January 16, 1920. Interestingly, after thirteen years of prohibition, Miller's TBU students did not share his opinion on prohibition. In a campus-wide poll in 1932, students were in favor of repealing the Eighteenth Amendment two to one.[11]

Alfred M. Reichard

Alfred M. Reichard, son of William and Elizabeth (Zeller) Reichard, was born on December 28, 1886, in Archbold, Ohio. He attended local schools in Archbold, graduated in 1909 from Davis Business College in Toledo where he learned accounting, and then went to Muncie, Indiana, to study teaching. He graduated from Marion Normal College (now a part of Ball State University) and later received his master's in accounting there. He also received a master's in pen art from Zanerian College in Columbus, Ohio. On August 13, 1921, he married the former Grace Neff; they had no children.

In 1909, Reichard answered an advertisement for an assistant principal position at the Ottawa Business College, which began his lifelong association with F. J. Miller. It was the first of two legendary letters that Reichard sent that changed the course of the future Tiffin University. Miller, after receiving the letter of application, was quickly impressed, noting that the letter was

most perfect in design, diction, and the most beautiful handwriting ever called to the attention of the recipient; an early interview was arranged, a teaching contract negotiated, and Professors Miller and Reichard were on a mutual teaching journey, starting in the fall of 1910.[12]

This was Reichard's first teaching assignment. He was well qualified for the job as an expert accountant and extraordinary master of the pen. A masterful teacher and academic, his teaching displayed why he later would become one of the most respected accountants in the Midwest. After two years in Ottawa, Reichard left to pursue his master's degree in Indiana. Miller loaned him five hundred dollars to help with tuition, secured by an insurance policy in event of his death, with a strong plea that he return in two years.

Both Miller and Reichard knew that the small town limited the growth of the school. In addition, commercial colleges in Lima and Findlay proved to be strong competition. Because of this, Reichard had little intention of returning to Ottawa after his studies were complete.[13]

Upon completion of his master's degree, Reichard sent his second legendary letter, asking Heidelberg University if his services were needed in their commercial college. The Heidelberg president replied that the business division was for sale. Miller and Reichard quickly seized the opportunity to purchase the school and were operating the Heidelberg Commercial College by 1912.

After spending six years together at Heidelberg, Miller and Reichard set off on their own to build Tiffin Business University. In November 1917, a few months after the move downtown, Reichard was drafted into the Army Air Corp. He had to leave their new venture for a two-year commitment in the army. Miller again wanted his friend to return after his tour of duty and promised him his position would be available upon his return.

The army drafted Reichard as a lieutenant in the 298th Air Squadron and used his teaching talents. First assigned to the Army Training Detachment in Cincinnati to instruct in radio work, military drills, and courtesy, he was later stationed as an instructor at the Carnegie Technical Institute in Pittsburgh and in a Schenectady, New York, installation.[14] He was honorably discharged in January 1919 and, since a

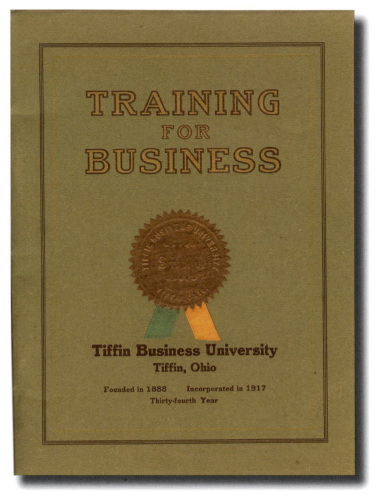

ownership at a bargain price to stay. However, Miller's friendship and loyalty, and his commitment to allow Reichard to invest in Tiffin Business University, drew him back. The party Miller threw the returning veteran was a true hero's welcome.[15]

Reichard was nationally known as an accountant and an accomplished handwriting expert. His principalship of the Accounting and Penmanship Department brought credibility to the young school. Reichard was one of only two college professors in Ohio to pass the Certified Public Accounting examination in 1922. The other professor taught at The Ohio State University. Miller was so proud of Reichard's feat that he declared a half-day holiday for the students upon receiving the news.[16] He was listed in the *Who's Who in Accounting* journal and published a text in higher accounting and auditing.

However, Reichard was most known for his masterful penmanship and handwriting expertise. He mastered every handwriting technique, including business script, writing script, ornamental writing, engrossing, and flourishing. Many of the most important diplomas, charters, documents, and certificates of the day were created with his hand. He charged one dollar a name to engrave diplomas. He engraved many diplomas not only in the region but also throughout the United States.[17] Law enforcement officials, who used handwriting analysis in forgery and other criminal cases, called upon Reichard frequently. His early work in graphology, the understanding of personality and character traits through one's handwriting,

married man had his position in Tiffin, he thought that he would see what was available in Schenectady. He chose to teach accounting and penmanship at Schenectady Business University and stayed until August 1919. It was a much larger business school than TBU and the only one in the city of more than 100,000; Reichard, however, wished to return to Tiffin. The owner of the Schenectady school offered him half

THE BEAUTIFUL IN PEN ART

PLAIN BUSINESS CAPITALS

TIFFIN BUSINESS UNIVERSITY, FULLY APPROVED

STYLES OF SCRIPT AND LETTERING EXECUTED IN THE UNIVERSITY PENMANSHIP STUDIO, AS USED ON DIPLOMAS AND CERTIFICATES

ORNAMENTAL SCRIPT

William J. Munson

OLD ENGLISH

MODERN TEXT

{Examples of Alfred Reichard pen art and penmanship. He was known as "one of the best penmen living today."[18]}

KOLLER'S, "THE BIG STORE," TIFFIN, OHIO.

was well received. He testified often in court. Most importantly, people simply enjoyed his handwriting presentations and pen art. Reichard would baffle crowds with his penmanship, often closing the demonstrations by writing people's names in the assembly backwards.[19]

Reichard shared Miller's ideals about practical, low-cost education. He too believed that education and hard work were the avenue to the American Dream. He shared the plight of the poor students who sought a commercial education. He had received no help from his family; he earned his education on his own. He often asked students to dig their way out of poverty by attending his school, sharing his struggle to earn an education: "I did not have any parent, grandparents, uncles, or aunts who ever contributed one dime, so I had to dig my way out of poverty to earn a good living."[20]

The Tiffin Business University Company

On December 10, 1917, at 9:00 a.m., on the Heidelberg campus, Franklin J. Miller held his last meeting as sole owner of the Heidelberg Commercial College and his first as the president of Tiffin Business University. Three days later, F. J. Miller and his fellow incorporators filed with the secretary of state of Ohio to become an educational enterprise called *The Tiffin Business University Company*. The articles of incorporation stated:

First. The name of the said corporation shall be The Tiffin Business University Company.

Second. Said corporation is to be located at Tiffin, in Seneca County, Ohio, and its principle business there transacted.

Third. The said corporation is formed for the purpose of establishing, maintaining and conducting an institution for the purpose of promoting education in all departments of business and commercial learning, knowledge and technic, especially in the subjects of Stenography, Bookkeeping, Typewriting, Banking, Accounting, Auditing, English, Composition, Penmanship, Salesmanship, Arithmetic, Commercial Law, Rapid Calculation and other allied and kindred subjects, to acquire and hold for said purposes money, real estate and other property necessary or proper to carry out said objects; and to do any and all things reasonable and necessary to be done to carry out said purposes.

Fourth. The capital stock of said corporation shall be Ten Thousand Dollars, ($10,000) divided into One-Hundred (100) Shares of One-Hundred Dollars ($100.00).[21]

In their first stockholders meeting on December 15, 1917, Miller was named president and Reichard was named secretary of the company. In addition, the stockholders promulgated regulations to operate the company. The Board of Directors was set at five members, and Miller exerted his command of the company by controlling the selling or transfer of stock. At that meeting, Miller inserted an article stating, "Before any interest in or stock certificate of this company can be sold, assigned, hypothecated, or transferred, such sale, assignment or transfer must be first approved by the President and Secretary of the Company."[22]

Miller's ten thousand-dollar investment in The Tiffin Business University Company was a hefty sum. He was able to amass the money from the profits of the Heidelberg Commercial College. He and Reichard agreed that they would only split from Heidelberg when they had the resources to be successful. They wanted to be sure they could purchase the best equipment and have sufficient working capital to advertise and produce an educational product that would separate them in the marketplace. From a financial perspective, Tiffin Business University was truly an F. J. Miller enterprise; nevertheless, he wanted his loyal academic partner A. M. Reichard to share in its profits. However, Reichard lacked the financial means to make a large initial investment. Miller committed to increase Reichard's stake in the venture over time. Of the ten thousand-dollar investment, six thousand dollars was used for working capital and four thousand dollars was invested in new equipment to make the third floor, and eventually the second floor, into a true classroom setting. New fixtures, desks, and business machines were added. TBU promoted itself as the best-furnished business school, a claim that went unchallenged. Few institutions of any kind invested a comparable amount in furnishings and remodeling at one time.

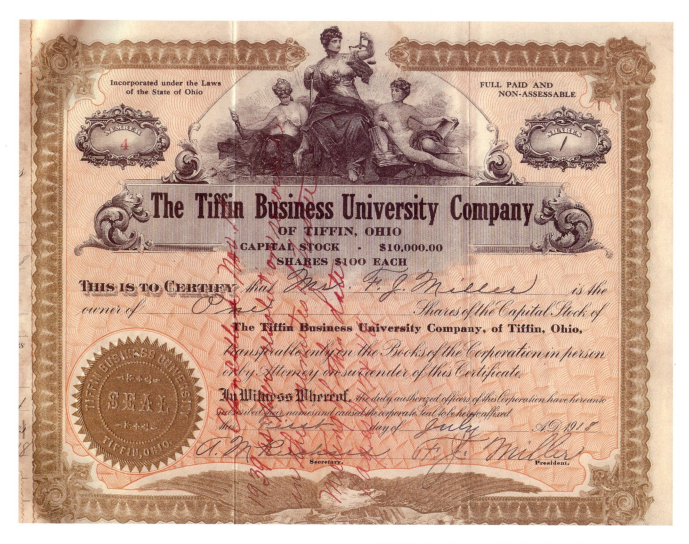

The secretary of state of Ohio accepted The Tiffin Business University Company incorporation documents on December 20, 1917. One hundred shares were offered at a value of one hundred dollars each. On July 1, 1918, Miller issued himself sixty shares. He also purchased a share each for his employees who came with him from Heidelberg: Reichard; Miller's stepbrother,

{*Certificate Number 4* is one of forty-three certificates issued by The Tiffin Business University Company from January 1, 1918, to January 8, 1930. The red vertical handwriting in F. J. Miller's hand says: *Cancelled November 18, 1939, as per resolution recorded in the minutes of Trustee Meeting of this date, pages 117 & 118.*}

{*Elizabeth Dryfuse*}

Guy L. Ewing; and Elizabeth Dryfuse. Miller's wife also held one share. Miller noted he was owed an additional thirty-six shares, which he said he would issue later. By Ohio law, five incorporators were needed to form a corporation. F. J. Miller, A. M. Reichard, Guy Ewing, Elizabeth Dryfuse, and Belvia Miller became the original incorporators of Tiffin Business University and constituted its first Board of Directors.[23]

Forty-eight stock certificates representing 273 shares of The Tiffin Business University Company stock were issued between 1918 and 1930. Eight individuals owned stock in the company throughout its history; however, Miller and Reichard always had the majority of the stock. Each share sold for one hundred dollars in 1918; that same investment would be worth seventeen hundred dollars today. Guy Ewing purchased an additional four shares during the first year. Ewing had taught stenography for Miller since 1912 and ran the night school in Fostoria from time to time. He was the first shareholder to sell his interest in the company. He sold his five shares on October 20, 1919, when he left Tiffin to work for Goodyear Rubber and Tire Company in Akron.[24] With Reichard's return from the military imminent, Miller was committed to increasing his friend's stake in the company. Reichard returned in time for the beginning of the 1919 academic year with money saved from his military service. He purchased nine shares of Miller's stock that year. That increased Reichard's ownership in the company to 13 percent. The new stenography teacher, Joseph N. Dell, purchased a share in 1920. After the first two years of operation, Miller owned ninety-two shares, Reichard ten shares, Elizabeth Dryfuse three shares, and Mrs. Miller and Joseph Dell each held one share.[25] Concurrently, Dell replaced Ewing as a board member.[26] Financially, these years were a success. Dividends were paid to shareholders, and bonuses were given to staff members.[27]

On September 29, 1920, the board of The Tiffin Business University Company voted to increase the capital stock from ten thousand dollars to fifty thousand dollars, divided in fifty shares of one hundred dollars each. They filed with the secretary of state of Ohio that day. It was quickly granted. In lieu of a cash dividend that year, the board voted to declare a 50 percent stock dividend and issued new stock on a pro-rata basis. Meanwhile, Reichard purchased an additional twenty shares from Miller; while Miller issued himself the additional shares he was owed. After the stock dividend and new purchases, there were 206 outstanding shares. Miller and Reichard owned 98 percent of the educational company, owning 78 percent and 20 percent, respectively.[28]

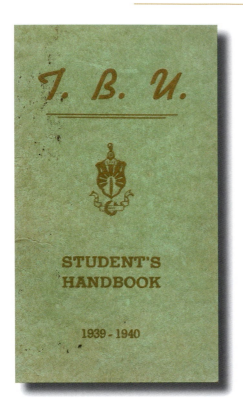

A few staff and friends of Miller owned a small number of the remaining shares. Elizabeth Dryfuse, who worked for Miller for more than ten years, resigned from the school and board in July 1925 in preparation for her upcoming marriage and move from the city. She accumulated five shares of stock through gifts from Miller and stock dividends over time. The company bought back the shares, and Miller presented her with a five hundred-dollar check at her going away party. Harry Taylor, who was a business partner with Miller in other ventures, including the farm, owned one share for seven years. Eugene Huth succeeded Joseph Dell in 1926 as the stenographic professor and purchased his three shares and Taylor's

one share. Huth purchased eight others between 1926 and 1930, increasing his total to twelve. Professor C. L. McKillip joined the university in 1925 and bought six shares from Miller over time. McKillip was named to the board in 1925 to replace Dryfuse, and Huth became a board member in 1926 to replace Dell.[29]

By the end of 1929, all of the trading and purchasing of stock was complete. The final percentage of ownership was Miller 72 percent (195 shares), Reichard 22 percent (58 shares), Huth 4 percent (12 shares), and McKillip 2 percent (6 shares).[30] Huth and McKillip became longtime and beloved teachers, both retiring from Tiffin University.

The "big four"—Miller, Reichard, Huth, and McKillip—shared an investment and a commitment to enlarge the university. They were compensated well for their investment. The shares paid generous dividends over the twenty years the company was in existence. Dividends averaged five dollars a share and one year paid as much as ten dollars.[31] This was in addition to the generous salary the officers of the company were paid. As officers, Miller and Reichard received $5,000 and $3,000, respectively, in the 1920s and $12,000 and $7,500, respectively, in the 1930s.[32] Miller's presidential salary would be $157,000 [33] today, a significant sum for a school of only 200 people in the 1930s. Fortunately, the four were never strictly concerned with matters of profit and operated the college as an educational enterprise devoted to students. They knew that one day Tiffin Business University would be better served as a non-profit enterprise.

End Notes

1   Tiffin Business University Catalogue, 1924.

2   F. J. Miller, *The Inception of the Idea, and Incidents Leading to the Founding of Tiffin University,* 1957.

3   Albert Keiser, *College Names and Their Origin and Significance* (New York: Bookman Associates, 1952).

4   Miller, *The Inception of the Idea.*

5   Ernst Hurst Cherrington, *The Evolution of Prohibition in the United States of America: A Chronological History of the Liquor Problem and the Temperance Movement in the United States from the Earliest Settlements to the Consummation of National Prohibition* (Westerville, Ohio: The American Issue Press, 1920), 353.

6   *Tiffin Daily Tribune and Herald,* August 6, 1918.

7   Sample Ballot. Election of Tuesday, November 5, 1918. This was given to the author by F. J. Miller's daughter.

8   Cherrington, *The Evolution of Prohibition,* 357, 364.

9   *Tiffin Daily Tribune and Herald,* August 6, 1918.

10 Harvey C. Smith, *The Annual Statistical Report of the Secretary of State to the Governor and the General Assembly of the State of Ohio for the Year Ending June 30, 1919* (Springfield, Ohio: The Springfield Publishing Company, State Printers, 1919).

11 *Tiffin Tribune,* November 4, 1932.

12 Miller, *The Inception of the Idea.*

13 *Tiffin Advertiser Tribune,* November 21, 1967.

14 *Tiffin Daily Tribune and Herald,* August 4, 1918, and January 17, 1919.

15 Ibid., August 23, 1919, and February 19, 1919.

16 *Tiffin Tribune,* November 3, 1922.

17 *Tiffin Daily Tribune and Herald,* May 21, 1920.

18 Tiffin Business University Catalogue, 1924.

19 *Tiffin Advertiser Tribune,* December 21, 1967.

20 Personal Letter from A. M. Reichard to Richard Pfeiffer, no date. This letter and other personal items from A. M. Reichard's life can be found in the Reichard Room in Seitz Hall on the Tiffin University campus. Of special note are displays of Reichard's pen art drawings.

21 Incorporating Document, December 10, 1917.

22 Minutes of First Stockholder Meeting of The Tiffin Business University Company, December 15, 1917.

23 Incorporating Document, December 10, 1917.

24 *Tiffin Daily Tribune and Herald,* November 8, 1919.

25 Stock Certificate Book. This book chronicles the stock transactions of The Tiffin Business University Company and contains the original stock certificates. Colorful stock certificates were issued and sold between 1917 and 1939.

26 Tiffin Business University Board of Trustees Minutes, December 31, 1920.

27 *Tiffin Tribune,* January 2, 1920.

28 Request to Increase the Capital Stock Document, filed with the State of Ohio on September 29, 1920. Also, see the Tiffin Business University Board of Trustees Minutes of September 29, 1920, and December 31, 1920.

29 *Tiffin Tribune,* February 5, 1926; see also the Stock Certificate Book.

30 Stock Certificate Book.

31 Tiffin Business University Board of Trustees Minutes, December 31, 1936, and June 10, 1938.

32 Tiffin Business University Board of Trustees Minutes, December 28, 1937.

33 Inflation Calculator: data.bls.gov/cgi-bin/cpicalc.pl

Chapter 8

The Remmele Block

When Tiffin Business University opened its doors to students that winter day in January 1918, it did so in the center of a growing and vibrant downtown Tiffin, Ohio. The Remmele Block, as the corner of South Washington and Madison streets was named, was at the epicenter of retail and commerce in Tiffin. Each of the twenty-eight steps to the second floor of this modern building represented access and opportunity, as dreams of escaping poverty filled the heads of students as they ascended.[1]

The university used the environs of a thriving downtown Tiffin to its advantage. The YMCA was within a few blocks of the Remmele Building and was used for physical education courses, recreation, and athletics. The Masonic Home was across the street and was used for dances and assemblies, as was the Knights of Columbus ballroom. For several decades, commencements were held at the Methodist Protestant Church, a block south on South Washington.[2] The Gibson Hotel, located just next door, served as a popular gathering place. The hotel's restaurant was named *The Green and Gold* and was committed to serving the more than two hundred students coming to and going from the Remmele Building daily. Students were admonished from time to time for playing the hotel's slot machines.[3] Trains and the interurban brought students to and from campus. Tiffin was a boomtown and the Remmele Block was bustling.

John A. Remmele

The Remmele Building was built by John A. Remmele (1834–1915),[4] a German immigrant and longtime local booster. John Remmele arrived in Tiffin penniless and lived to amass a fortune. He borrowed sixty-four dollars to secure a sixty-nine-day voyage from Germany to New York. After the difficult journey, he came directly to Tiffin in 1852 at the age of eighteen. The Tiffin he arrived in was a town of five hundred people. Although having no schooling in Germany, he learned the meat butchering trade there and immediately found work in Tiffin for four dollars a month. He almost succumbed to the 1854 cholera outbreak and later survived typhoid fever. He befriended a variety of local businessmen who taught him business skills and financially backed him throughout his life. In 1855, Horace Huber loaned him enough money to start his own butchering business on the present site of the Remmele Building. After making $150 the first year, he struggled for several years until he began

STORE OF C. F. HANSBERGER & CO.

{The First Public Rendering of the Remmele Building. This building was the home of Tiffin Business University from 1917 to 1939 and Tiffin University from 1939 to 1956, used to promote the new location of the C. F. Hansberger & Company Department Store in the *Souvenir Program Commemorating the Seventy-Fifth Anniversary of the Founding of the City of Tiffin, (1822–1897).*}

purchasing real estate, always borrowing from local boosters instead of from a local bank. In 1866, he purchased a yellow brick building and a few old buildings on the corner of South Washington and Madison. This footprint constituted the future site of the Remmele Block. Thirty years later, he demolished all of these buildings to construct the largest and most modern building in Tiffin.

Remmele was prompted to build by an offer from Charles Hansberger, with the promise of a ten-year lease to house his department store. Financially backed by Samuel B. Sneath, John Remmele began construction in April 1897, and C. F. Hansberger and Company opened their 17,000-square-foot venture only six months later as the self-proclaimed *Greatest General Store in Northwest Ohio.*[5] Hansberger lauded it "as the best lighted and largest building for commercial reasons in Tiffin."[6] The rent from the department store covered his costs, and the second- and third-floor leases made him a wealthy man. John Remmele continued to build more downtown structures and play a prominent role in the development of Tiffin until

his death in 1915. Remmele's son-in-law, William H. Hopple, managed the building for the estate after his death.

The Remmele Building

The Remmele Building, designed by F. K. Hewitt, was an imposing structure. The upper floors of this building were home to Tiffin University from 1917 to 1956. The building fronted South Washington Street, the main street of Tiffin, with 60 feet and ran 180 feet west on Madison. The first floor was built with stone and the second and third floors were brick with stone

trim. A stately tower completed the building. The first floor, always designed as a retail center, was occupied by a large department store. Harold's Department Store was the longest tenant of the building during the university's tenure, anchoring the building from 1934 to 1955.

On February 7, 1918, an open house was held to introduce the Tiffin community to the remodeled third floor of the Remmele Building as the new home of Tiffin Business University. Miller charged architects McLaughlin and Hulsken of Lima, specialists in educational building, to redesign the upper floor.[7] The university began with four classrooms and grew to ten rooms by 1922, occupying more than ten thousand square feet of the third floor. By 1924, they occupied the entire second and third floor, adding a social hall, equipped with a large stage, and more classrooms and offices. Miller leased the building for $140 and enjoyed a fair relationship with the property owner, W. H. Hopple. They argued about repairs and rent from time to time, but they always resolved their differences.[8]

The Library Expansion

F. J. Miller and A. M. Reichard were on track to grow the small commercial college into a real university. The natural next step was junior college status. The college, in many ways, held status and accreditations beyond what was required by the Association of Junior Colleges of America. TBU raised entrance requirements, had a qualified and growing faculty, and enjoyed annual surpluses in revenue. Most importantly, it was one of the few business schools authorized to award bachelor's degrees. One final requirement stood in the way: a library. The school had amassed twelve hundred loyal alumni, and school spirit was strong. Miller received ten to twenty letters weekly from satisfied alumni. He felt the time was right to embark on the institution's first fundraising effort: to establish a library in the Remmele Building and stock it with four thousand volumes. This was a bold move, since it was still a for-profit institution.

On March 8, 1926, Miller announced this campaign to the community.[9] This first capital campaign endeavor sought to raise six thousand dollars to ensure

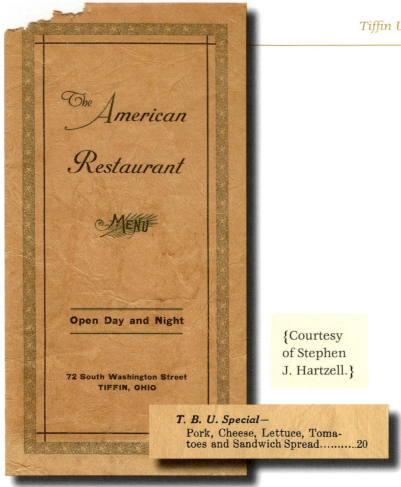

Open Day and Night

72 South Washington Street
TIFFIN, OHIO

T. B. U. Special—
Pork, Cheese, Lettuce, Toma-
toes and Sandwich Spread..........20

on April 7, 1926, and remodeled quickly thereafter.[11] A year later, the university expanded into two small rooms formerly occupied by the G. A. R. and the Clinton Township Trustees. The rooms were combined into one spacious reading room, sometimes called the literary room.[12]

The TBU Farm

By the beginning of the third academic year at the Remmele Building, enrollment growth allowed the university to have a strong balance sheet. Miller began investing surpluses in the stock market and real estate. He invested heavily in converting the upper floors of the Remmele Building into a well-appointed college building. However, talk turned to the possibility of building a traditional campus with green space.[13] The first step was to purchase land. The Tiffin Business University Company in 1921, with the help of Harry Taylor, purchased a 119-acre farm in Clinton Township on North State Route 53. The community knew it as the TBU Farm or the University Farms well into the 1960s. President Miller was motivated to do this on two distinct levels. At one level, he felt the school needed its own campus one day to survive, and the farm's location was ideal. He believed, on another level, that he should have marketable assets available to back up his investment in the educational business venture to ensure that he could recoup his investment and allow the school to continue after his death. The farm was purchased on January 19, 1921, for $19,500.[14] Just the year before, Miller's capital stock value was

the complete expansion throughout the second floor of the Remmele Building. The small but loyal group of stakeholders responded. The present students and staff raised three thousand dollars: two thousand dollars to remodel the literary hall and one thousand dollars for new books. The Class of 1926 added five hundred more volumes as a class gift. Alumni organized nationally for the first time and raised enough to fully subscribe the campaign. Within a year, Tiffin Business University raised seven thousand dollars, exceeding their goal.[10] The new library was dedicated increased to $17,000.[15] The farm, leased to local farmers, provided a modest income for the university over time. The university struck oil in 1929 and operated an oil well on the property for some time.[16] Along with a few stocks, the farm made up the bulk of the endowment the school claimed to establish. The farm played a historic role in the life of the university and the Tiffin community. It would play a major part in the institution's move to non-profit status and the city of Tiffin's aviation history.

End Notes

1   Interview with Paul Deppen.

2   *Tiffin Advertiser-Tribune*, June 1, 1933.

3   *Tiffin Advertiser-Tribune*, November 28, 1934.

4   John Huss, *Tiffin Advertiser-Tribune*, April 6, 2003.

5   Ibid.

6   *Souvenir Commemorating the Seventy-Five Anniversary of the Founding of the City of Tiffin, 1822–1897* (Akron, Ohio: The Werner Company, 1897).

7   Tiffin Business University Catalogue 1924.

8   Tiffin Business University Board of Trustees Minutes, July 11, 1934.

9   *Tiffin Daily Tribune and Herald*, March 8, 1926.

10 *Tiffin Tribune*, June 12, 1927.

11 *Tiffin Daily Tribune and Herald*, April 7, 1926.

12 *Tiffin Tribune*, April 15, 1927.

13 Personal story of F. J. Miller.

14 Seneca County, Ohio Deed Records, Vol. 190, page 136.

15 Request to Increase the Capital Stock Document, filed with the state of Ohio on September 29, 1920.

16 *Tiffin Tribune*, September 3, 1929.

17 *Tiffin Daily Tribune*, April 23, 1923; Lisa Swickard and Tricia Valentine, *The Extremists: Tiffin Seneca County Living History*, Vol. 4 (Tiffin, Ohio: Virgin Alley Press, 2001), 9; conversation with Charles Ardner.

{Before TBU occupied the whole second and third floors, they shared the building with local professionals and others. At the height of the xenophobic 1920s, the Ku Klux Klan set up headquarters on the second floor to stand against the burgeoning Catholic immigrants of Tiffin, especially the Italians and Irish. On August 8, 1923, while the police were at the county fair, the Klan burned six crosses in Tiffin, although the one at Sycamore and Monroe failed to light. Their intimidation and attacks were short lived in Tiffin. Citizens rallied and joined police in the resistance, often taking up arms on their own.[17] Citizen Victor Ardner accosted a Klansman in the stairwell of the Remmele Building at gunpoint and impeded his continued attacks. The gun used is shown here.}

{State, National, and World Championship Medals of Adella Shedenhelm Myers. The fastest and most accurate typist in the world.}

Chapter 9

Academic Life

When Miller and Reichard started their first academic year on the third floor of the Remmele Building in 1917, the world was at war. They began in an atmosphere of optimism, goodwill, and patriotism. They quickly adjusted their curriculum and schedule to meet the needs of those preparing to serve. Concurrently, Miller and Reichard began to reassess the total academic standing of the school, hinting that it would offer four-year degrees. Tiffin Business University, as had the Heidelberg Commercial College, began offering one- and two-year programs in higher accounting, business administration, and secretarial studies; short courses in stenography and typewriting; night school; and other short programs in civil service–related subjects that prepared students for the civil service examination.

Tiffin was considered stronger than most commercial colleges of the day and offered many collegiate amenities. The quality of the institution was judged both internally and externally by how well its graduates secured meaningful and well-paying positions. The institution, as Miller and Reichard had fashioned it, was perfectly adapted to the needs of business education and the times. To their credit, they also realized that the school could not survive without changing to meet the new conditions of an established academic society. These times, the 1920s, held quick, forceful academic curriculum changes. Tiffin Business University's offerings would be dramatically altered, going from offering diplomas to bachelor's degrees in just one decade.

Commercial College to Junior College

Since the early 1910s, the legitimizing seal of academic accreditation was sweeping the American higher education landscape. Some order was needed to quantify higher education and stop emerging diploma mills. Different institutions, providing different services, added to the confusion. Educational quality was questioned. Normal schools, commercial colleges, professional schools, traditional four-year colleges and universities, and junior colleges all joined together to provide education. However, each held different standards and expectations. In addition, competition from colleges, high schools, and junior colleges forced the old-time commercial college to raise standards. The North Central Association (NCA) was the most prestigious of the new accrediting agencies and had high standards. The biggest hurdle they imposed was not academic but financial: requiring a half-million-dollar endowment in 1924. For this reason, many Ohio colleges had difficulty securing NCA accreditation in the early part of the century.[1] Fortunately for Miller and Tiffin Business University, business school, state association, and junior college accreditation developed concurrently and presented a challenging and yet more realistic accreditation path for TBU than the NCA.

Natural business planners, Miller and Reichard assessed what was needed to secure every possible official recognition for their small school. They understood that securing accreditation from the established business associations and actively participating in new groups would advance the school. Internal policies were changed to match accrediting standards. Each success was aggressively marketed. Few people realized that Miller and Reichard had such resolve.

A year after they moved downtown, Tiffin Business University was placed on the accredited lists of business schools by the National Association of Accredited Commercial Schools, an association founded in 1912.[2] This was a first in a series of differentiating events that would slowly separate them from other commercial colleges. This association authorized Miller to organize the similar Ohio commercial colleges into a state association.

The first twenty-five years of the twentieth century saw a marked increase in high school attendance and graduation resulting in a need for more teacher training. Most normal schools were not prepared to serve the increased need to certify commercial teachers for high schools. Miller saw an opportunity. Tiffin Business University sought state of Ohio approval to train and certify teachers in this field. As an early member and leader of the Ohio Business Schools Association and the Ohio Commercial Teachers Association, Miller worked tirelessly with the State of Ohio Department of Education to help fashion high standards that would allow his school, and a few others of similar quality, to certify teachers in Ohio. The two-year commercial normal school course in education was approved in 1923, and it evolved into a state-approved three-year program in 1927. The state was eager to offer an official certificate to Tiffin Business University to train commercial teachers on a four-year basis on January 4, 1928. This was an outstanding and necessary educational accomplishment for the young college, putting them on the same plane as other four-year teaching programs in Ohio.[3]

Concomitant with the state of Ohio's teacher training recognition of Tiffin Business University, the state added a few commercial colleges to its official college accreditation list. Ohio was progressive in its commitment to commercial education[4] and wanted to demonstrate that, of the more than forty commercial colleges operating in the state in 1930, seven were of a higher standard. The following letter was sent to all of the state's school district superintendents and college presidents:

Columbus: *Bliss College;*
                   Office Training School
Dayton: *Miami Jacobs College*
Tiffin: *Tiffin Business University*

The private Commercial College exists in Ohio at different levels of quality. The seven schools listed here have undertaken, however a meritorious project in the standardization of a two year or four year program in the technical fields of commerce. Each one continues to function as a regional trade school in one of its divisions of the school and seeks to meet increasingly high standards adapted to the college level in the course of the next few years. For this reason, these schools are worthy of special mention to you as private commercial schools of the college level. Of course, they are not in any sense, solely teacher training institutions. The seven institutions are:

Cleveland: *Spencerian School,*
                    Dyke School of Commerce,
                    Wilcox School of Commerce.

These are the only private commercial colleges on any accredited list of this department at the present time.[5]

It was not surprising that Miller immediately launched a statewide advertising campaign and commissioned a new catalog to articulate the distinction. It was significant that of the seven schools selected by the state for accreditation all but one was located in Ohio's largest cities. Tiffin Business University was the only one located in a city with fewer than 100,000 in population. Many fewer for that matter, as the 1930 U.S. census placed Seneca County's population at 47,951 and Tiffin's at 18,495.[6] Miller and Reichard's development of the school in a small market is quite impressive.

The State of Ohio

Office of

Department of Education

By virtue of the authority vested in the Director of Education by the statutes of the State of Ohio in the acceptance of credits for the issuance of teaching certificates, I hereby certify that ___Tiffin Business University___ of ___Tiffin___, Ohio, following inspection of work and approval of program, is rated as a teacher training institution which is authorized to offer the following curricula and to grant credits for the successful completion of the same.

Commercial

This certificate shall remain in full force and effect until revoked by the Director of Education or until it is superseded by a later certificate issued by the same authority.

In Testimony Whereof, I have hereunto subscribed my name and caused my official seal to be affixed, at Columbus, the ___twenty-seventh___ day of ___December___ in the year of our Lord one thousand nine hundred and twenty-___seven___.

Director of Education

{The state of Ohio granted authority to Tiffin Business University to award the degree of bachelor of Commercial Science on December 20, 1924. It later approved the granting of teaching certificates recognized in thirty-three states.}

Upon starting Tiffin Business University, Miller and Reichard abandoned the practice of accepting and allowing students to begin at any time and quickly adopted a traditional academic calendar. The academic year was a semester system with the fall semester beginning in September and the spring semester beginning in late January. A six-week summer session usually began in June. Students were in class all day taking seven courses. The school offered one-, two-, and four-year programs during this time. As Miller and Reichard improved the academic standing of the school, most one-year programs were dropped. Those that remained did not lead to a diploma or a degree.

The American Association of Junior Colleges officially recognized Tiffin Business University as a member in 1926. It was one of the first officially recognized junior colleges in Ohio.[7] Rider College of Trenton, New Jersey, the University of Southern California, and the University of Chicago were the first institutions to accept transfer student credit for TBU's first two years.[8] By 1930, twenty-three required courses and nineteen elective courses were offered annually. Seven full-time and three part-time instructors taught these courses. In addition to business-related subjects,

TBU offered courses in religion, physical education, economics, psychology, salesmanship, law, public speaking, and sociology.[9]

The Curriculum

The one-year business curriculum that Miller and Reichard brought from their Heidelberg days was a rolling program; students could start at different intervals and times throughout the year. After the penmanship course, the students moved on to the bookkeeping course. Students would only move on to the next course when they satisfactorily mastered the work and passed an exam. Students had to pass a rigorous comprehensive examination before receiving a diploma, and just as important, Miller's full attention of job placement services. Miller's placement activities became legendary to graduates of TBU and potential employers. The curriculum and education delivered were designed for successful job placement. Tiffin Business University offered one-year programs suited for quick training and placement for some time. Students could choose a one-year specialization in secretarial duties, bookkeeping and accounting, and specialized civil service training, mainly in typewriting and stenography. President Miller personally counseled these students and assessed what type of business work best suited them. He ensured that they would receive a job offer upon completion. Most of the one-year students received civil service positions, many at a high wage. Over time, the one-year programs were phased out, although they were periodically offered when the marketplace demanded them, and if Miller saw that specialized training was needed, he provided it.[10]

Two-Year Program

The two-year program in higher accounting and business administration was the university's first strong academic program and was the foundation for securing junior college status. By the opening of the 1920–21 academic year, all diploma programs were two years in length. Students could choose between the accounting and business administration program, the executive secretarial program, or the commercial normal course, newly approved by the state of Ohio. Only those in two-year programs received diplomas, and a strong distinction was made between training in the one-year program and academic work

in the two-year program. Commercial education in the 1920s became a significant offering at the high school level, replacing what earlier commercial colleges offered. While some commercial colleges could survive this movement, Miller and Reichard used this change as an opportunity to upgrade their two-year program and add normal school education courses to their curriculum.

Civil Service Program

Since the passage of the Pendleton Act of 1883, employment in the federal government or civil service was increasingly based on merit to combat the entrenched spoils system. The act established the Civil Service Commission and developed an increasingly sophisticated and decentralized testing mechanism for employment for entry-level government jobs. From 1883 to 1900, 10 to 13 percent of new employees who were selected for government service through this method had some college training, and commercial college education was the primary provider of education for new federal employees during this period.[11]

The most important component for securing a government position was the Civil Service Commission examination. The presidents of the Progressive era, especially Theodore Roosevelt, William Howard Taft, and Woodrow Wilson, increasingly advocated for merit selection of federal workers and sought to increase compensation and benefits. The gradual improvement in testing was so well accomplished that it became possible to administer an examination locally in almost every required field. During this time, with the onset of World War I, the influence and size of the federal as well as state bureaucracy increased and, in turn, markedly increased the need for trained workers. In addition, throughout World War I, women were employed for the first time in vast numbers as secretaries and clerks. At the height of World War I, 75 percent of the new federal appointments under the civil service laws were women. Veteran preferences were a part of civil service reform since the Civil War. However, they were intermittently enforced, and veterans were poorly served. This mistake would not be repeated after World War I. Veteran preferences were fully enforced, and by 1934, a quarter of the federal workforce was veterans.

President F. J. Miller understood these national trends. He fashioned his curriculum and marketing to serve those who sought to secure a government position. For some time, Miller marketed the Tiffin Business University education as a vehicle to pass the civil service examination and to step up to a middle-class job. He taught to the test. Night school was steadily offered since he purchased the school from Heidelberg in 1912. He did this partially in response to the market forces and partially to fend off the thought of someone opening a competing school. Appealing to working adults and returning veterans, he offered classes from October to April, two nights a week from 7:00 to 8:45 p.m. Concentrated offerings in stenography, typing, business administration, accounting, and auditing made up the curriculum. Miller boasted of the quality

and efficiency of the educational experience. A high percentage of TBU graduates took the civil service examination in Tiffin and directly entered government work. Fifty dollars in tuition secured a fifteen hundred-dollar-a-year job.[12] Many women graduates went directly to Washington, D.C., upon completion, and veterans of World War I enrolled in high numbers.

By 1922, Miller was well acquainted with the needs of the Civil Service Commission and the employment opportunities of the nation. For example, the civil service test for railroad mail workers was particularly difficult, and the job was highly desired. Miller created a short one-year course to help students pass the test and secure an immediate sixteen hundred-dollar-a-year salary working for the postmaster on the rails. The program was a success for many years, and Miller marketed the program with a class slogan: *No failures, and no appointments under $1600.*[13]

As events leading to World War II intensified, so did the need for more trained workers for civil service. Miller organized special classes at the beginning of the 1940 academic year for potential civil service workers. The Civil Service Commission authorized Tiffin Business University to conduct the examinations in their classrooms for positions in Ohio and in Washington, D.C. Separate examinations were offered for men and women. For example, the typist examination for women wishing to earn $1,440 a year was one day and the men's senior stenographer examination to earn $1,620 a year was the next day. Miller announced the testing dates well in advance to

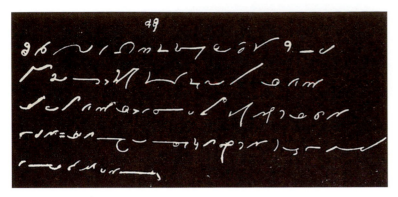

encourage both enrollment in his program and successful tests results. He kept close ties with the commission for his school and country. Congressman Dudley White worked closely with Miller to advance civil service education.[14] President Miller made several trips to Washington, D.C., and met with the commission directly. He explained this program in an article in the local Tiffin newspaper:

The U.S. Civil Service Commission thru (sic) the medium of letters, bulletins, and personal calls from representatives of the commission has to induce and lend encouragement to the officials of Tiffin University young men and women to enter government service, through the medium of civil service as a part of the national defense program. The examinations will be conducted in the T.B.U. regular classrooms.[15]

Commercial Normal Course

Since 1888, many of the graduates from the Heidelberg Commercial College taught commercial education in the common schools and high schools of the area. Certification was often awarded after an examination, and a degree was not needed. By 1920, the state of Ohio required two years of normal school or commercial education and a state certificate to teach commercial education in public schools. Most normal schools were not equipped to offer commercial education and a few progressive commercial colleges quickly added education as an offering. Tiffin Business University was one of the first in Ohio to offer certification in commercial education. The state wanted strong proficiencies in penmanship, typing, and stenography. TBU's well-appointed typing and office equipment rooms, along with innovative stenographic and typing instruction and Reichard's reputation as an outstanding penmanship instructor, made TBU well suited for this endeavor. Miller strengthened his program by adding the highly regarded educator, Charles A. Krout, to instruct the teacher training classes. Krout later became the Tiffin city school superintendent, and C. A. Krout Elementary School in Tiffin is named in his honor.[16]

TBU's teacher education program enabled its graduates to teach in any four-year Ohio high school, as well as those in thirty-five other states. One of the first of its kind in the United States to receive authority to educate secondary school business teachers, graduates of the TBU commercial normal course received a teaching certificate awarded by the State of Ohio Department of Education.

Bachelor of Commercial Science

Miller and Reichard's ultimate aim was to offer a traditional four-year degree. In 1924, the university applied to the State Department of Education for authority to confer a bachelor of commercial science degree with majors in higher accounting and business management, and commerce and finance. This authority was quickly granted, and four graduates in the Class of 1925 were the first to receive a bachelor's degree. The commercial normal course was also elevated to a bachelor of science in education degree. The state sent the following authorization:

This certifies that authority is hereby granted to Tiffin Business University, under the provisions of Section 9923 of the General Code of Ohio, to grant the degree Bachelor of Commercial Science, (B.C.S.) to graduates on the following basis:

1. Graduates of Higher Accounting and Business Administration course who complete eighty-four semester hours of residential work as filed with the department, and who have had three years of experience, appraised by the President of that institution as worthy of twelve semester hours of credit per year.

2. To only those graduates of the approved, first grade high school.

3. To those graduates of the Commercial Normal course who complete ninety-six semester hours of resident work requiring attendance of two regular years (18 months), and three summer terms, and twenty-four semester hours of additional credit earned at least six months of practical office or teaching experience appraised by the president of the institution as worthy of that amount of credit.

The above institution has satisfied the requirements of section 9923 with respect to the filing of the Secretary of State.[17]

Eventually, the final year of practical work was dropped and a full 120 hours of academic work was required to earn the bachelor of commercial science degree. The ability to offer a bachelor's degree was a seminal event.

End Notes

1 James A. Hodges, James H. O'Donnell, and John W. Oliver. *Cradles of Conscience: Ohio Independent Colleges and Universities* (Kent, Ohio: Kent State University Press, 2003).

2 *Tiffin Daily Advertiser,* February 12, 1919.

3 *Tiffin Tribune,* January 5, 1928.

4 Ibid., November 6, 1930.

5 Ibid., January 14, 1930.

6 United States Census Bureau, *The Census of the United States of America, 1930.* Use of the United States Census Bureau website (www.census.gov) is also very helpful.

7 *Tiffin Advertiser-Tribune,* February 19, 1934.

8 *Tiffin Advertiser-Tribune,* May 5, 1933.

9 *Tiffin Daily Tribune and Herald,* December 14, 1932.

10 Tiffin Business University Catalogue, 1919.

11 Paul Van Riper, *History of the United States Civil Service* (Evanston, Ill.: Row, Peterson, 1958), 165.

12 *Tiffin Tribune,* October 11, 1919.

13 Ibid., February 4, 1922.

14 *Tiffin Advertiser-Tribune,* October 7, 1938.

15 Ibid., August 24, 1940.

16 *Tiffin Tribune,* February 4, 1922.

17 Tiffin Business University Board of Trustees Minutes, June 1924.

29

$$H^{20} + C^{20} + P^{20} + P^{20} + CS^{20} = SUCCESS$$

Health + Character + Purpose + Preparation + Common Sense = SUCCESS.

30

Disloyalty and Poor Work may injure your imployer, but it will ruin you.

31

Scatteration is the curse of the hour to the American life.

32

Don't loop the loop of social activity or down town amusement every other night and expect to attain any marked degree of personel efficiency in your educational preparation this year.

If you want a ...
keep after it ...
get it some da...

---

20. Egotism
21. Disloyalty
22. Wasted Hours
23. Vacillation
24. Dishonesty
25. Lost Opportunity

I

What I am to be I am now becoming.

2

1 Plan
2 Prepare
3 Push
4 Prayer

3

Preparation is the Golden Gate th...
leads to the city of success.

4

...e without a purpose is like
...p without a rudder.

5

...can be done.

6

...e hand of your life ...
...e era of pr...

Salesmanship and Business Efficiency

1.

Sept. 24,1936-This year of school shall help to determine what my future life shall be.

2.

...o searching for the nuggets of gold ...at lie hidden in your own life.

3.

...rsonality Requisites:

Character	6. Disposition
Health	7. Curtesy
Appearance	8. Observation
Mannerism	9. Ambition
Attitude	10.Christianity

4.

...esmanship is the Power to Persuade
...spects to Purchase our Product
...a Pleasure or Profit Producing
...oposition.

8

You can't wabble and win.

9

As you pass along lifes highway, keep your eyes and ears open.

10

As we do, so we be.

11

Pick your duck.

12

Use your backbone; not your wishbone.

13

Sow a Thought and reap an Act;
Sow an Act and reap a Habit;
Sow a habit and reap a Character;
Sow a Character and reap a Destiny.

14

Salesmanship is the Power to Persuad...
People to Purchase our Product at
a mutual Profit.

SUCCESS REQUISITES

1. Good Health
2. Christian Character
3. Pleasing Personalit...
4. Definite Purpose
5. Thorough Training
6. Willingness to Work

SECRETS OF FAILURE

1. Deficient Education
2. Poor Personality
3. Hereditary Tendancies
4. No Definite Aim
5. Carelessness
6. Dissapation
7. Inertia
8. Wrong Attitude
9. ...rofligacy
10. ...d Investments
11. ...Initiative
12. ...k of Common Sense
13. ...k Character
14. ...ility To Sell One's...
...iced.
15. ...y Marriage
16. Devoid of Appreciation
17. Impatience
18. Poor Health
19. Atheism

{The renowned aphorisms of F. J. Miller, as captured by Ivan Cole, Class of 1938.}

Chapter 10

The Miller
Educational Philosophy

F. J. Miller was a hard-driving, no-nonsense educational entrepreneur. He, at times, was a dichotomy. He could be both dramatic and controlled. He was a businessman and an educator. He was autocratic and benevolent. He was opinionated, yet open to new ideas. He was deeply influenced by his early years of teaching in rural Hancock County, knowing his own meager teaching salary and seeing experienced teachers unable to afford to purchase a house. He saw the new career field of business as much more lucrative. He coupled his love of teaching with his desire to make a comfortable living and turned them into a career as a purveyor of commercial education. For his entire life, Miller's livelihood depended on how well he recruited, educated, and placed students. These three attributes, coupled with his desire to select the type of students that he felt industry wanted, molded his educational philosophy.

Aggressive Advertising and Recruitment

In contrast with traditional colleges and universities of the day, Miller's success in enlarging the institution must be attributed to, in large measure, two factors: advertising and recruitment. Miller's vigorous and sustained public relations program involved heavy media advertising, and his student recruitment plan became so perfected that it was a part of the culture of the school. Every member of the staff was expected to recruit. This included an exhausting round of personal appearances, speeches, home visits, high school performances and visits, and relentless telephone follow-up. Miller paid generous bonuses to faculty and staff who helped recruit students, and the bonus was increased for recruiting valedictorians and for students hailing from out of state.[1]

Miller's advertising campaign focused on securing lucrative employment upon graduation. He was not shy about how he said it. His aim was for graduates to make money. TBU purchased weekly display advertisements and placed articles lauding the salaries that graduates were receiving. Every placement, every job secured, was reported in the newspaper; if it was not reported in an article of detail, then it appeared in the *Sixty Day Employment Report*. This *Sixty Day Employment Report*—a quarter-page display advertisement placed in the lo-

{TBU Class of 1932. Hazel Anderson upper right.}

cal newspaper every other month from 1912 until well into the 1960s—became legendary in the Tiffin area. The report would list the name, hometown, employer, position, and most importantly, the graduate's salary, under the headline *Try the T.B.U. Way to Permanent Employment and Regular Pay* in the paper.

Often, Miller and his recruiters would ask the prospective student how much money he wanted to earn upon graduation. After the student answered, Miller would point to the report showing the student some-

one from his hometown earning more than the student expected. The report was widely distributed, and as the Depression dawned, it became more important. Students could not wait to see their name in the paper with their new salary listed for all to know. Often, alumni promoted themselves to the university, and their new salary was published in the next employment report. Securing a job for fifteen hundred dollars in the height of the Depression was paramount to striking oil for poor local students.

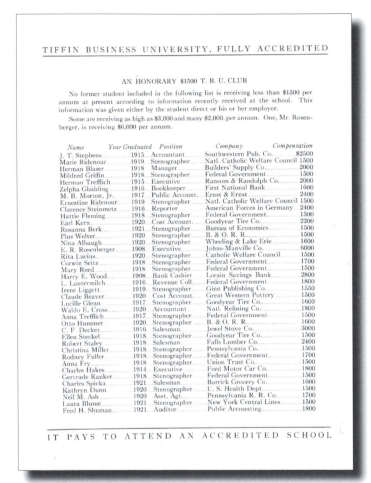

enrollment grew a phenomenal 65 percent.[2] This 5 percent decrease in four-year college enrollment, while not devastating, left eighty thousand young men and women either looking for work or seeking alternate education opportunities. The movement grew steadily since 1912 and peaked in 1927. At the onset of the Depression, more than five hundred junior colleges were operating, many in previously underserved markets.[3]

The Depression aggravated several educational conditions that already existed. First, many families found it increasingly difficult to finance attendance at traditional four-year institutions. Second, finding work became more difficult, if not impossible, and employment required training that was more specialized. Third, high school graduation doubled during the 1920s, serving as a catalyst to a general social change that included a prolonged education, and more education at all levels (high school, junior college, and four-year programs) was reaching social and economic classes

TBU and the Depression

A report commissioned by the American Association of University Professors (AAUP) in 1937 titled *Depression, Recovery and Higher Education,* drafted by Malcolm Willey, sought to evaluate the impact of the 1929–1935 Depression years on higher education. It reported that traditional four-year college and university enrollment decreased 5 percent during the Depression, while junior college and technical school

{TBU basketball, 1951. African-Americans, Jewish-Americans, Protestants, and Catholics joined together on this team. Dave Rosen and Calvin Dilworth said TU offered them opportunities when others didn't. Left to Right: Othmar Frank, Gene Conrad, Calvin Dilworth, Al Linhart, Jim Stull, Omar Tolsen, Arlen Addis, Dan Benham, Keith Corbin, Dave Rosen, Coach Dick Routh, and Manager Howard Collier.}

previously not served. Malcolm Willey summed up his five hundred-page report to the AAUP in these few words, "The Depression served to reemphasize the opportunistic nature of the growth of higher education."[4] The increased need of access to inexpensive, regional, employment-driven education was an outgrowth of the Depression, and nobody knew this better than Tiffin Business University President F. J. Miller. He seized the opportunity.

Miller used the Depression to his school's advantage. When many traditional colleges and universities were retrenching, Miller increased his advertising and marketed his practical education philosophy directly against the liberal arts curriculum. He began increasing his rhetoric in public appearances and writings, often directly stating,

A high-grade secretary can more easily obtain employment at present than a Greek scholar, or one who holds a general degree only. Specific training in some definite field, carried to a high degree of qualification, is paramount in obtaining employment today.[5]

He discussed that higher learning in the United States was ill defined and his education philosophy was more practical. As enrollment grew and Miller's personal financial position became firm, he became more aggressive in articulating this view. He felt Tiffin Business University gave form and body to a new American institution delivering the kind of education he believed the times demanded. He editorialized in the local paper:

Why does not someone define just what is Higher Learning? There are thousands in the U.S. who never attended an institution of Higher Learning, including Lincoln, Henry Ford, Edison, and the Wright Brothers. There are thousands today carrying Excess Baggage who have never scored, made good, or rendered any service to their community. Suppose a young man goes through college—any type of college, and has not been taught to work, or is dishonest, what do degrees signify? This is not against, or the fault of degrees. The question is merely asked, When is one educated? The writer holds two degrees, but is unable to answer the question.[6]

Miller increased his marketing efforts to sell his philosophy. He hired a full-time recruiter to recruit outside the local area. Miller's recruiting representative traveled eight thousand miles the first year. Generous scholarships were offered for the first time in 1933 to valedictorians or salutatorians, and by 1935, a fourth of the class held that distinction. Most chose the institution for its job-placement prowess.

Capacity Enrollment Brings a New Selectivity

Tiffin Business University was at capacity by 1935. Enrollment figures showed that it was still a regional school, with half the student body matriculating from Seneca County.[7] Many students, nonetheless, came from as far west as Idaho and as far south as Florida. Students transferring from other colleges became commonplace, and many students sought a business degree after already holding a bachelor's degree from other institutions. The student body reflected the region, and most were of modest means and limited backgrounds. As more out-of-town students matriculated, boarding

T B U REGISTRATION FAR AHEAD OF '35

School Bars Overweight, Laggard Students

houses sprang up in Tiffin to meet the new demand. Women students, in exchange for room and board, often cared for children and performed domestic work.[8]

There is no evidence that Miller and Reichard ever were prejudiced against women or minorities. However, there were few minorities in the Tiffin region. While at Heidelberg, they encouraged the Cuban nationals to attend, and their admissions policies were always co-educational. The first African American student of record was Hazel Anderson of Sandusky, Ohio, Class of 1932, who became a teacher in Missouri after graduating. Pauline Alexander was the first African American employee of the university. Miller was proud of her appointment in his school and feted her to the community.[9] He asked Alexander, a former student, to stay after graduation to gain collegiate teaching experience. She went on to teach at Wilberforce and Bethune-Cookman universities.

As a waiting list developed in the late 1930s, so did Miller's desire to become more selective, albeit through a path not usually chosen. Miller and Reichard were always interested in pleasing the industrial and business community by placing accomplished graduates in their employ. At times, they customized their curricula offerings to meet the needs of industry. For example, Reichard developed two classes in the Ford Corporation accounting method, which Ford encouraged, and in turn, the company employed many accounting graduates from TBU.[10] As an outgrowth of his philosophy and rhetoric, Miller became fanatical about the work ethic of students, as well as their personalities, their appearances, and their ability to be placed in employment after graduation. He began to formulate admissions standards to effect a change that would include very personal attributes. In the local paper, he awkwardly expressed his new philosophy to the community. The headline read: "T. B. U. Registration Far Ahead of '35—School Bars Overweight, Laggard Students." Miller was not subtle in his articulations:

Four types of applicants are being refused admission; those who are exceedingly overweight; those who are exceptionally tall or diminutive in stature, combined with personalities precluding the possibility of ready employment; those with physical impairments of a nature that renders placement impossible; those who ranked in the lower third of their graduating class scholastically.[11]

President Miller was quite comfortable promoting his new admission requirements. He fiercely believed that he was in concert with industry and the business world. Miller said he considered it unfair and unethical to accept students who did not have at least a fifty-fifty chance of finding employment. He realized that:

much criticism will be voiced against this new standard in education even though it is in a highly specialized field but that he was firmly of the conviction that thousand of misfits in life vocationally can be avoided by this method, and that the day will come reasonably soon when this plan will be followed quite universally by the better types of colleges, universities and technical trade schools such as T. B. U.[12]

Miller used these standards for some time, although he eventually abandoned them when enrollment waned during World War II.

End Notes

1 Tiffin Business University Board of Trustees Minutes, June 7, 1939.

2 Malcolm MacDonald Willey, and the American Association of University Professors, Committee Y, *Depression, Recovery and Higher Education,* 1st ed. (New York: McGraw-Hill Book Company, 1937), 263.

3 Leonard Vincent Koos, *The Junior College* (Minneapolis: University of Minnesota, 1924).

4 Willey, *Depression, Recovery and Higher Education,* 484.

5 *Tiffin Advertiser-Tribune,* February 2, 1933.

6 Ibid., October 11, 1935.

7 Ibid., September 21, 1934.

8 *Tiffin Tribune,* June 28, 1930.

9 *Tiffin Advertiser-Tribune,* April 12, 1935.

10 Ibid., February 15, 1938.

11 Ibid.

12 Ibid., August 7, 1936.

Chapter 11

Student Life

Tiffin Business University thrived in its downtown Tiffin location. A true college was developing in the comfortable, albeit small, quarters of the Remmele Building. Unlike most institutions of higher learning in the 1920s and 1930s, its campus occupied two floors of downtown office space.

Despite the limited size of the campus, a student life program, reflecting a great measure of sophistication, developed. Students enthusiastically arrived, undaunted by its lack of pastoral green space, and they created a sense of student life and campus spirit that truly shaped the institution. Even without much legroom, Tiffin Business University added many four-year college features and student enhancements, including athletics, fraternities and sororities, literary societies, music programs, a college paper, and many other social activities. These programs provided outward signs of progress and prosperity to the community by being well reported in the local newspapers.

Symbols of school spirit quickly arrived. The college colors used at Heidelberg of white and maize were abandoned, and green and gold gained the status of official school colors.[1] In 1925, George Lepard wrote the first school song with Velma McDowell serving as composer.[2] The song was based on the emotions of those bidding farewell to their college.[3] Mrs. Wade K. Chamberlin introduced the first *Alma Mater* magazine in 1931, and a scene depicting two college students seated in a canoe illustrated the cover. Christmas of 1912 marked the first homecoming dance. The dance became a popular annual celebration, and as many as a third of the twelve hundred alumni returned annually to join students and faculty at this celebration.[4] An additional Tiffin tradition began in 1933 with the first Parents' Day, another way to keep parents apprised of college events.[5]

A Student Council was created in 1923; it quickly became an influential body charged with "all questions affecting the welfare of the student body or the general interest of the school."[6] Issues were decided by the joint vote of the students and faculty. President Miller was highly democratic in giving voting power to students, and he encouraged debate.[7] Students and faculty met in luncheon conferences to discuss campus issues. Students voted to extend the Christmas vacation from one to two weeks, and Miller and the trustees obliged.[8]

Music Programs

Music played an important role in the life of Tiffin Business University. In September 1919, the college organized its first orchestra and glee club. The orchestra became quite accomplished, growing to more than fifty members under the longtime direc-

{The orchestra under the direction of Joseph Schares, with Professor E. H. Huth as faculty manager. The Symphony Orchestra held numerous public performances throughout the year, including an annual Christmas program on WSPD Radio of Toledo.}

tion of Professor Joseph Schares. It toured local high schools, performed at service clubs, and held annual concerts.[9] President Miller used the orchestra as a recruiting and public relations tool, securing publicity for the young school.[10] He masterfully secured public broadcasts of the orchestra on WSPD radio in Toledo and WAIU radio in Columbus.[11] Trios, quartets, and soloists were also featured, and a graduate, Neva Ruth Ames, was recruited after one of these performances to join the Major Bowes Amateur Hour. She toured with the group for many years and also performed on Broadway.[12] Vocal music groups were also popular. Tiffin Business University sponsored a mixed chorus, men and women's glee clubs, and a concert choir. Elise Weidling directed the vocal programs until her death in 1929. Mrs. Wade K. Chamberlain succeeded her as director of the department. At one time, a third

of the student body were members of one of the musical groups.[13]

Religious Life

Tiffin Business University was clearly a for-profit proprietary educational institution, neither affiliated with nor controlled by any religious group or denomination. Yet, that fact did not preclude it from sponsoring religious activities. Miller and Reichard were deeply religious, but not rigid men in their faith. They wanted to offer religion as a character and moral guide for their students. The decade after World War I was a time of social testing of traditional norms and values. Miller and Reichard believed that the business community was more likely to hire employees who had a strong moral code and some religious training. Miller and Reichard were nondenominational in their presentations to students. Often the weekly assembly speaker would be a religious person, and Jewish, Protestant, and Catholic speakers were equally represented.[14]

Miller started holding a weekly Chapel Assembly in the tradition of denominational colleges. It was called a chapel program in the early years, but by the mid-1920s, it had evolved into popular assembly programs with an opening and closing prayer and always a well-done musical selection. The early commencement speakers were often clergymen.[15]

An overall sense of religious respect permeated the campus with social activities suspended during Lent. Accomplished religious leaders of all faiths spoke on campus and TBU offered religious courses as electives. Sixty-five students registered for the Reverend Paul Hollingshead's religious education class in 1935. This optional class was offered in the evening for some time and was well attended.[16]

F. J. Miller's long association with the Seneca County Sunday School Association enabled Tiffin Business University to offer classes in Religious Leadership Training for church and Sunday school teachers throughout the region beginning in 1928.[17] The five courses of instruction were offered for many years and met in the evening once a week.[18]

Assembly Program

The assembly program became a major part of campus life and played a crucial role in developing a progressive and open communication between students and faculty. President F. J. Miller communicated well with students, and he used the assembly program to foster school spirit and communicate campus information. Every Friday, an all-campus assembly took place. Well organized, entertaining, and informative, it was popular with students and faculty. President Miller usually welcomed the group and imparted his wisdom and philosophy to the gathering. He became well known for his aphorisms at these assemblies. Students took many of these maxims to memory, and most alumni from Miller's era can still recite his phrases.

The assemblies sought to make well-rounded students out of those from modest backgrounds. The assemblies included prayer and musical arrangements from the university orchestra or glee club, or from an accomplished outside group. New members of Greek-letter organizations or athletic teams were recognized or honored at these functions. The program was the highlight of the assembly, which was typically a speaker of some renown or a local civic leader. Students heard personal development speakers such as local medical doctors, religious leaders, and executives of industry. At times, faculty entertained, fraternities put on plays, literary societies performed musical numbers, and sororities announced campus dances. Interesting speakers of note who were invited back numerous times included H. Dana Hopkins of the Heidelberg Speech Department, Coach Sayger from Heidelberg, and YMCA Director A. G. McQuate. John Freidman, president of National Machinery Company in Tiffin, was a frequent speaker and was often accompanied by his son Robert, who, as an eight-year-old composer,

{Left: Richard Pfeiffer, Jean Pfeiffer, Olive Paramenter, Mary Huth, Marygene Huth, and Eugene Huth at the Harvest Dance.}

{Above: Doris "Ma" Benner at the Spring picnic.}

THE TYSTENAC

We'll See You There

DANCE

OCT. 29

MASONIC TEMPLE

D. WARD

performed his original music. Robert Friedman would return often to perform musical scores on his accordion and other instruments. He and his wife, Eugenie, became major benefactors of Tiffin University in the 1990s.

Student Newspaper

Throughout the 1920s, student newspapers were published informally. A new student-run newspaper was established in 1935. *The Tystenac*, named for *TY* from typing, *STEN* from stenography, and *AC* from accounting, started with more than fifty students and became a very well-read and prestigious college newspaper.[19] President Miller introduced it to the community saying that it "not only would afford students valuable training in journalistic English and composition, but will also provide excellent practice for typing, mimeograph and the business side of the newspaper."[20]

{Fraternity Hell Week, 1955. Tiffin University featured an active Greek Life since 1922. Their service and antics were popular in Tiffin.}

Fraternities and Sororities

Debating teams and literary societies were the first Greek-letter organizations to emerge at Tiffin Business University. Informal groups of professors and students gathered since 1918 to discuss current events, sing songs, produce informal plays, and socialize. Both founded in 1922, the Athenian Literary Society and the Delta Literary Society developed into the first two literary societies at Tiffin Business University. These two societies, interestingly, were founded as co-educational organizations, and faculty members were also members. Forensics, theatre, debate, and reading books from the new library were early activities. The academic contributions from the literary societies were invaluable for a new institution. They played major roles in helping the university establish a library and remodel the literary room in the Remmele Building, which served as their meeting place. Their main contribution, however, was that they were primarily social clubs. The Delta and Athenian literary

{Students of the university roomed in private homes throughout Tiffin. F. J. Miller advertised that "many of the best homes in Tiffin, situated in the best residential districts are open to T.B.U. students." A typical student paid $1.50 to $2.00 a week, which included heat, light, bath privileges, and laundry. The restaurants of Tiffin also vied for the students' business, providing weekly meals at reasonable costs, often 25 and 35 cents a meal.}

societies held campus-wide dances, provided speakers for assemblies, and held debating tournaments. They often hosted joint meetings and social functions. Since the university did not sponsor any housing for students, the literary societies were important social and academic outlets for the students and fostered a strong campus spirit. Two additional literary societies were added in 1936: Alpha and Epsilon Nu Omicron. The four literary societies were combined into two co-educational groups in 1939: the Delta–Alpha Literary Society and the Athenian–Ep Nu Literary Society.[21]

The establishment of Greek-letter organizations reflected a notable change on campus. Their value was endorsed by the administration, and they were quickly recognized as approved student organizations. Student life did not center on fraternities and sororities; most of the time they were open organizations that augmented student life. When college-wide dances were held, a sorority would help with decorations and a fraternity would assist in providing refreshments. Sigma Omega Sigma Fraternity in 1924 and Theta Sigma Chi Sorority in 1925 were among those organizations. Kappa Delta Phi Sorority and Alpha Iota Sorority were added in the 1930s.

The Board of Trustees understood that the presence of Greek-letter societies both enhanced college spirit and raised concerns. The administration supported, yet closely monitored, the societies. Paddling was prohibited in the 1940s, but certain hazing practices were acceptable. The following account portrays an innocent, though interesting, look into hazing at the university in the late 1920s:

The boys have gone through a great deal the past two weeks such as no talking with the girls or no dates; proposing to strange women; running errands; walking; fishing from man holes; wearing baby caps; and worst of all no shaving.[22]

Miller liked the fraternities and sororities on campus, and he met often with the leadership of the groups and enjoyed attending their events.

The first secret honorary fraternity revealed its members' identities and explained its purposes in the Friday assembly program on May 15, 1936. The fraternity, Delta Sigma Kappa (DSK), was organized four months earlier for the purpose of honoring students possessing qualities of scholarship, leadership, character, and ability to serve. The identities of members are revealed only once a year. Russell Witter founded the honorary fraternity that still exists today.[23]

Athletics

Under the new colors of green and gold, Tiffin Business University continued to offer basketball as a sport, as it did at Heidelberg. Sponsoring an athletic program was important to Miller and Reichard. They sought to add as many college amenities and spirit boosters as possible to add distinction to their emerging institution. As with the *Heidelberg Commercials*, the new TBU teams played club teams across northwest Ohio. For the first ten years, their opposition included area high school teams such as Thompson, Old Fort, Bettsville, Green Springs, the Junior Home, Sycamore, St. Wendelin of Fostoria, and St. Ann's of Fremont. A member of the team usually held the dual role of player and coach. The team used the Junior Home Auditorium as their primary home court from 1919 to 1930. During the 1930s, TBU used the St. Joseph gymnasium, the YMCA, and the Tiffin Junior High School gymnasium as their home courts.

President Miller was proud to offer basketball for both men and women. The women's basketball teams were well reported in the local papers and often were more successful than the men's teams. Tiffin Business University women's basketball squad of 1922 was undefeated.[24] The 1924–25 women's team was also undefeated and claimants of the Northwest Ohio Girl's Basketball Championship. Miller boasted in the *Tiffin Tribune* that the "old belief that athletes are not good students was shattered, all of my starting five are 'A' students."[25]

Accomplished coaches were hired beginning in 1926. Ralph Gust, who studied under Knute Rockne, wanted to attend business school as well as develop his coaching skills. He was hired with the incentive of free tuition and one hundred dollars to coach basketball with a goal to upgrade the program.[26] He fielded interesting and exciting teams and was the first to add collegiate teams to the schedule. Findlay and Bluffton colleges were added in 1927, as well as St. Johns of Toledo, which boasted a schedule including Toledo University and the University of Detroit. Fans in Tiffin enjoyed his colorful players, especially Red Johnson, one of the best players in Northwest Ohio who happened to be a midget.[27] His teams were the first to be truly competitive, going 14–3 during the 1926–27 season and 8–3 during the 1927–28 campaign.

Gust developed the baseball program in 1928. Baseball games were scheduled sporadically at League Park and Rhodes Field[28] in both the spring and the fall. The team's opponents included the few high schools that offered the sport. The baseball team played in the area's spirited semi-professional league in the summer, as well as competing against the strong single "A" team from Tiffin, the Tiffin Mud Hens.[29] After completing his business training at TBU in 1928, Gust

{Coach Ralph Gust studied under Knute Rockne, upgraded the basketball program, and started baseball in 1928.}

briefly coached at Bucknell University and later went into banking in Fremont, Ohio.[30] After Gust resigned, the basketball teams were led by a series of coaches of local athletic skill and fame, namely Pop Hall, C. M. Hook, Dwight "Stick" Haley, and Charley Bridges.[31]

Tiffin Business University's high school schedule, from 1929 to 1934, was popular with the students and the community. It was easy to recruit area athletes; anyone who enrolled was eligible to play.[32] Rules gov-

{Front row: left to right: Archi Welch, Blair Patterson, Gene Ringholz, Tom Conrad, and Howard Williams. Middle Row: Coach Keller, Dale Walcutt, Allan Haines, Gregory Schroeder, James Lonsway, Donald Shutt and Manager John Lloyd. Back Row: Ralph Korb, Harry Close, Charles Clements, (future TU President) Richard Pfeiffer, Wayne Riedel, Charles Stout, and Harry Van Voorhis.}

THE TIFFIN BUSINESS UNIVERSITY

ATHLETIC ASSOCIATION

by action of the Board of Trustees and Faculty

certifies that

Eugene Berlekamp

on account of Meritorious Service in

VARSITY BASKETBALL

has been granted this Certificate of Merit

Tiffin, Ohio
March 1, 1935

DIRECTOR OF ATHLETICS

PRESIDENT

SECRETARY

MANAGER

erning competitions were organized; however, as was common in the day, teams would put someone in the line-up who was not a student. For example, when Eden High School's coach started as pitcher in a baseball game, TBU countered with their coach taking the mound.[33]

Charley Bridges, who also coached for free tuition, brought new athletic innovations.[34] His 1934 basketball team became the most successful team in the school's history and the first to beat the Junior Home kids.[35] He started tennis in 1934, and it was played intermittently throughout the 1930s. Intramurals strengthened with fraternity and sorority athletic competitions that were well reported in the local papers.[36] Bridges also organized a popular table tennis league with Heidelberg, the YMCA, and National Machinery. The annual ping-pong tourney was often the lead sports story in the *Advertiser Tribune* newspaper.[37]

Coach A. Ray Keller, a graduate of the university, became a member of the staff in the early 1930s as an instructor of accounting, and he became the baseball coach in 1932.[38] He was selected in 1934 to succeed Bridges in basketball and led the entire athletic program. He immediately began to upgrade the athletic programs, both at the intramural and varsity level. Well-liked and imbued with school spirit, Coach Keller worked hard to involve as many of the two hundred-plus students in some kind of athletic competition as

he could. Throughout most of the 1930s, Tiffin Business University fielded only two sports at the varsity level: basketball and baseball. Keller coached both and taught accounting as well. He also ran the assembly program and the intramural activities. The varsity opponents were still an eclectic mix of local high school, college, and community club teams. Keller was determined to eliminate non-college teams from the schedule and to upgrade the program's visibility and quality.

Keller successfully founded the Indiana Ohio Athletic Conference in 1939. Tiffin Business University was a charter member along with Giffin Junior College of Van Wert, Ohio; Urbana Junior College of Urbana, Ohio (later to become Urbana University); and Indiana Tech in Fort Wayne. Later, Defiance, Cedarville, and Rio Grande from Ohio and Taylor College in Upland, Concordia of Fort Wayne, and Tri State in Angola, Indiana, joined the conference. The schools associated because of their similarities: Giffin, Tiffin, and Urbana sponsored mostly two-year programs, and Indiana Tech, a school of two thousand students, was an engineering school that condensed a four-year baccalaureate degree into two years. The Indiana Ohio Athletic Conference did not include football.[39] By 1940, TBU's basketball and baseball teams no longer played any competition other than that of collegiate rank.[40]

The Indiana Ohio Athletic Conference was a success in the region and allowed both Tiffin Business University and its fellow conference members to make significant athletic advancements. Playing only college teams brought noteworthy recognition to the university in the community. The season of seventeen basketball games often included Toledo University.[41] Attending Tiffin University's basketball games became popular in Tiffin and successful season ticket sales ($2.00 for adults; $1.00 for students)[42] helped cover the majority of the team's expenses. TBU won the league's first conference championship in 1940.[43] Athletics were firmly established under Keller, further separating the institution from a commercial college and moving closer to traditional American colleges.

Keller also augmented the already-popular intramural bowling program with horseback riding and archery, and he also added golf as a varsity sport.

The school colors, green and gold, established in 1917, became standardized under Keller. While red was added occasionally, Keller insisted that all uniforms be green and gold, avoiding the past temptations to use class colors or to take what was available from the local supplier.[44] Due to the lack of an official moniker, the teams acquired many different nicknames over time. The early development of college nicknames and mascots in the United States often arose from a local sportswriter's reference to the teams,[45] and this was the case in the early days of TBU. They were most often referred to as "the Bookkeepers." At times, they were called "the Accountants," "the Remmele Block Collegians," "the Businessmen," "the Kellermans," and "the Commercials."[46] Both men's and women's teams were called "the Stenographers" from time to time; however, this was usually reserved for the women.[47] Yet, this tradition would soon change in the next decade. A contest to officially adopt a nickname was sponsored by the student newspaper, *The Tystenac*, in 1941; and after a vote of the student body, the "Dragons" emerged as the victor.[48]

End Notes

1 *Tiffin Daily Advertiser,* February 14, 1918.

2 *Tiffin Tribune,* April 3, 1925.

3 *Tiffin Advertiser-Tribune,* May 20, 1932, and *Alma Mater* of Tiffin Business University. The *Alma Mater* in 1932 was as follows:

In college days, when all is gay
And life but at the start
There comes to each a love supreme
Awak'ning in the heart;
And when we ask "What is this love,
This first love fond and true?"
From many hearts the answer rings,
"'Tis dear old T. B. U."

To thee dear school, Our T. B. U.
Out in the world may we prove true
Ever remembering, never forgetting
Our love for you, dear T. B. U.

Our college and its memories
Will come to us each day
And life with all its joys and cares
Can ne'er drive these away;
Our hopes and prayers and fairest dreams,
Our friendships, staunch and true
All center round our first great love,
Our dear old T. B. U.

4 Christmas Homecoming Dance Program, December 19, 1929. *Tiffin Tribune,* December 19, 1930. F. J. Miller printed elaborate programs for his dances.

5 *Tiffin Advertiser-Tribune,* March 28, 1936.

6 *Tiffin Tribune,* September 23, 1923.

7 *Tiffin Daily Tribune and Herald,* November 4, 1932.

8 *Tiffin Advertiser-Tribune,* November 28, 1934.

9 *Tiffin Tribune,* November 15, 1929 and *Tiffin Advertiser-Tribune,* February 26, 1935.

10 *Tiffin Advertiser-Tribune,* August 9, 1934.

11 Ibid., February 25, 1932, and May 8, 1936.

12 Ibid., December 20, 1937, and February 17, 1939.

13 Ibid., March 28, 1936.

14 Ibid., October 21, 1938.

15 Ibid., March 24, 1932, and October 11, 1935.

16 Ibid., February 11, 1938.

17 *Tiffin Daily Tribune and Herald,* December 17, 1932.

18 Ibid., January 4, 1932.

19 *Tystenac,* October 1935.

20 *Tiffin Advertiser-Tribune,* February 4, 1935.

21 Ibid., April 20, 1939.

22 *Tiffin Tribune,* October 18, 1929.

23 *Tiffin Advertiser-Tribune,* May 15, 1936.

24 *Tiffin Tribune,* February 4, 1922.

25 Ibid., March 14, 1925.

26 Ibid., July 11, 1927.

27 Ibid., December 2, 1927.

28 *Tiffin Advertiser-Tribune,* April 13, 1934.

29 Ibid., May 2, 1939.

30 Ibid., November 10, 1936.

31 *Tiffin Tribune,* September 30, 1929, and May 16, 1928.

32 Ibid., December 22, 1939.

33 Ibid., October 19, 1935.

34 Ibid., October 28, 1931.

35 *Tiffin Advertiser-Tribune,* March 3, 1935.

36 Ibid., January 5, 1937.

37 Ibid., October 13, 1936, and April 9, 1936.

38 Ibid., April 13, 1934.

39 Ibid., September 30, 1940.

40 *Tystenac,* April 1939; October 1939; and May 1939 Issues.

41 *Tiffin Advertiser-Tribune,* December 2, 1940.

42 *Tystenac,* November 1939.

43 Ibid., February 28, 1940.

44 Ibid., March 1940 and November 1939.

45 Mark T. Jenkins, *Nickname Mania: The Best college Nicknames and Mascots and the Stories Behind Them* (Conway, Ark.: Admark Communications, 1996) and Ray Franks, *What's in a Nickname?: Exploring the Jungle of College Athletic Mascots* (Amarillo, Tex.: R. Franks Publications Ranch, 1982) tell an interesting story on the development of college nicknames in America.

46 The athletic teams were well covered in local and college papers. As was the early college custom, many college nicknames evolved from names repeatedly used by newspaper reporters. Interesting examples of this for Tiffin University can be seen in *Tystenac,* June 1939; *Tiffin Tribune,* January 23, 1931; *Tiffin Advertiser-Tribune,* February 25, 1935, and March 4, 1940.

47 *Tiffin Tribune,* January 10, 1931.

48 Personal interview, Russell Sorg.

{The Paradiso Athletic Complex, with the Tiffin University Nature Preserve easily visible on a fall day. Courtesy of Jeremy Croy.}

Chapter 12

A University Grows
into Its Name

On January 27, 1938, Tiffin Business University celebrated its fiftieth anniversary. Franklin Miller invited the community to an open house to note that "commercial education has been offered in Tiffin since 1888 . . . this being the fiftieth year of continuous service to youth and the community."[1] The college had grown far beyond a typical commercial college of the day. It was both a junior college and an institution empowered by the state of Ohio to grant four-year degrees. In addition, it held a small but substantial endowment, and had no debt. The Remmele Building reached its 250-student capacity, and as a result, a waiting list developed. The institution was clearly a for-profit institution since its inception in 1888, providing an educational product dedicated to customer satisfaction. However, few students and community members saw it solely as a for-profit corporation.

Nineteen thirty-eight would become a watershed year for the owners and the institution. By then, Miller and Alfred Reichard had owned the institution for more than a quarter of a century, building a personal financial asset and a successful educational enterprise. Understandably, they both wanted it to be preserved. Early in the year, Professor Charles McKillip, with Miller's blessing, set off for Pennsylvania to own and operate his own commercial college. As he had done with Reichard, Miller promised McKillip that he could return to his old position at any time, and he did in short time. However, McKillip sold his six shares of Tiffin Business University company stock to Miller.[2] This left Miller, Reichard, and Eugene Huth

the sole remaining owners of the outstanding stock of Tiffin Business University. The three devised a plan to pay themselves for their stock and to perpetuate the institution after their deaths. They spent the remainder of the year conducting their affairs as if the institution was a non-profit university, concurrently investigating tax laws and financial avenues to fund their investment.

Miller's intentions were not simply eleemosynary. He valued his share of ownership in excess of twenty thousand dollars and Reichard's of at least eight thousand dollars. They wanted to cash in their stock if they were relinquishing ownership of the school. Becoming a non-profit institution was a secondary benefit and a way for them to receive their funds. Their choice was to either sell to outside individuals or use the surpluses or assets of the school to recoup their investment. Selling to an outside source, although, was clearly a fateful act. Miller flirted with outside investors, but he wanted to retain control, and his best option was to use existing assets. Consequently, Miller and Reichard concocted a plan to exchange the TBU Farm for their stake in the institution, but changes in the Internal Revenue Service code spoiled the plan. A vote of the Board of Trustees in 1937 to transfer the land to Miller and Reichard was rescinded when legal counsel informed them that exchanging the land at no cost violated federal corporate law. Ironically, legal counsel for the school advised Miller that

if Tiffin Business University was a non-profit entity, they could legally exchange the property for their interests. They accepted the decision and agreed to go non-profit. By exchanging their stock for promissory notes, Miller decided to put off compensation until a later date.[3]

After a year of conducting its affairs in a non-profit manner, the Board of Trustees voted unanimously on November 10, 1939, to perpetuate the ideals and purposes of Tiffin Business University as a non-profit institution. The resolution emphasized:

Whereas, it is the aim of this organization to conduct its affairs in accordance with the principles which are recognized as essential to maintaining the highest standards apropos to educational institutions of collegiate rank, and

Seitz Hall Steeped in History

Present-day Seitz Hall is steeped in Tiffin lore—tracing its origin to some of Seneca County's earliest settlers and the area's most devastating fire. Milton and Maria (Gregory) McNeal arrived in Fort Ball by horseback in 1823. They lived in the block house of the Fort until they readied their wood-framed store with living quarters upstairs at the busy corner of Sandusky and Miami streets.

Their general store served Fort Ball, Tiffin, and the surrounding rural area with dry goods, clothes, preserved foods, and hardware. Milton would stock the store from his annual trips to the East, traveling by horseback to Cleveland and then by rail to New York. During one trip around 1830 he contracted cholera and died along the way. Maria boldly took over the store and ran it successfully, with their son Austin, for more than fifty years.[4]

Early afternoon on April 13, 1872, Maria was mixing lye and lard in a large kettle directly over a fire stoked with dry hickory wood. Her normal day of soap making turned tragic when the sparking hickory wood mixed with a northeastern gale. The fire ignited in her summer kitchen and in thirty-eight minutes it traveled a half-mile to the Washington Street Bridge, burning everything in-between.

The Great Fire of 1872 destroyed seventy buildings along Miami and Monroe streets, Frost Parkway, and almost a block on North Washington Street.[5] A newly purchased Adriatic steam fire pumper, called the Seneca Chief, saved the day, stopping the fire from jumping the Sandusky River and taking out the central business district north.[6]

Maria and Austin used their insurance money to rebuild, albeit in brick this time. It was run as a neighborhood grocery, as Motry's and Rumschlag's well into the 1960s. It was sold to TU in 1968 and became Seitz Hall in honor of alumni Paul and Marian Seitz on November 12, 1987. Paul and Marian used to shop at McNeal's.

Whereas, the corporation now has no indebtedness, and there having been created a small endowment or surplus and there being no dissenting shareholders, nor preferences, in favor of any creditor shareholder,

Now, therefore, in order to inaugurate and perpetuate the principles, ideals, and purposes on which the institution was founded, That of Service to Others Without Profit, Be it resolved that each and every shareholder shall surrender his or her shares to the corporation for cancellation, and thereby release all rights, privileges and powers which the holders of said shares heretofore enjoyed.[7]

Their petition to the state of Ohio for non-profit status included a new set of bylaws for the institution and a new name: Tiffin University. For-profit Tiffin Business University was to become independent: the non-profit Tiffin University.

What's in a Name?

Although many Ohio college enrollments shrank during World War II, Tiffin University's swelled when it answered a call from the federal government. In 1943, the War Department was in dire need of trained typists, stenographers, and clerical workers. Because of Tiffin University's reputation as a first-class business school and its approximation to Wright Field in Dayton, it was selected as the only institution in the Midwest to train more than eight hundred women for the Air Technical Service Command (ATSC). The ATSC sought trained personnel for material command to keep the U.S. Air Force supplied with resources, especially parts, bombs, planes, food, drugs, and clothing.

Wright Field in nearby Dayton was one of the largest logistical centers for the Air Force, and the male clerks normally doing these duties were deployed elsewhere in the war effort. The Air Force sought trained women to fill these jobs.

This highly selective, intense program lasted fourteen weeks with classes running six days a week, eight hours a day. Students came to Tiffin University from ten states. An immediate, generous salary, paid tuition and textbooks, and automatic placement at Wright Field upon successful completion of the rigorous program added to the students' desire to serve their country at a time of war. Without this program, it is questionable whether Tiffin University could have survived the war; it provided 90 percent of the institution's income.

At the same time, there were few men on campus. Coach Keller suggested suspending the varsity basketball program, as tire and gasoline rationing exasperated the prospect of playing out of town. The athletic funds were not lost, however; the college offered bowling, archery, and other gym activities in lieu of intercollegiate sports.[8]

Miller and Reichard survived the war years, albeit they and the institution did not emerge with the same energy of the past. Miller and Reichard sought to recoup their investment by selling the farm and airport, and retirement was being considered. Miller reduced his pay for the first time to six thousand dollars (seventy-two thousand dollars today)[9] in 1945 and was awarded an honorary doctor of Commercial Science

that same year from Tiffin University.[10] The road to non-profit status was not immediate or easy for the new TU. For the first time, the school did not throw off excess cash as it had done in the past, slowing the ability to pay off the notes. Miller added a new board and faculty member, Robert (R. A.) Morton, who brought much talent to the university, but it was clear he was promised more. Miller convinced him to purchase Reichard's six thousand-dollar note so Reichard would be free to retire; Morton believe he was buying a personal stake in the enterprise. In the early 1940s, the institution stopped filing tax returns, resulting in an audit by the Internal Revenue Service.[11] The IRS found nothing serious: TU needed to increase its board members from five to seven, pay some taxes, and officially wind-up the business by paying off the notes of sitting board members. Morton insisted there was a side deal with Miller for him to take full control and ownership; eventually he bought Miller's notes and believed the notes would give him control. Briefly, a debate about

the efficacy of non-profit ensued; however, Miller and the others stood firm.[12] Miller offered a four thousand-dollar gift for needy students with the condition that the institution remained non-profit. The IRS audit as well as an internal review showed some irregularities in Miller's previous payments, resulting in overpayment, which were resolved.[13] However, its strongest

{The "Campus in the Clouds."}

case for finishing up the move to non-profit status came from one of the board's soft-spoken members, Eugene Huth.

As now secretary, I had nothing to do with the making of the agreement of which Mr. Morton spoke as having with Mr. Miller, knew none of its provisions and that it was purely a personal matter between Mr. Morton and Mr. Miller and Mr. Miller to adjust. I feel that if no financial interest were held by anyone that Mr. Miller, the alumni or anyone else, would feel more inclined to make gifts, contributions, or money available to worthy students as loans and that these would not be enjoyed by the college as long as financial interests were held. He also said that he felt the combined judgment of a Board of Trustees would be more valuable to the college than if one or more individuals had financial interests and therefore would expect more influence given their views.[14]

Although it took a decade to finally work out all of the financial dealings and pay back its investors, Tiffin University emerged as a real non-profit institution, ensuring its movement toward the dawn.

Reichard remained actively affiliated with the institution for thirty-five years as secretary of the Board of Trustees and principal of the Accounting Department until he retired in 1947. President Miller, in education since 1900, announced his retirement on June 10, 1953, and was named president emeritus in honor of his forty-one years of service. The four key leaders of Tiffin University—McKillip, Huth, Reichard, and Miller—had longevity of service as well as life. Charles L. McKillip, kindly known as Mac, was affiliated with the

school for more than fifty years and died at the age of eighty-eight. Eugene M. Huth, associated with the university for fifty-eight years (1918–1976), died just short of his ninety-third birthday. Alfred M. Reichard lived to be nearly eighty-one years old. Franklin J. Miller's longtime phone exchange at the university, known to many in Tiffin, was 905. Miller died at 9:05 p.m. on September 1, 1976; he was ninety-six years old.[15]

The board chose one of its own, Richard C. Pfeiffer, to succeed Miller as president. Pfeiffer often commented that he was chosen because he was the only member of the board who lived and worked in Tiffin. An alumnus and successful accountant, Pfeiffer quickly hired the university's first academic dean, Dr. Olive Paramenter, to offset his lack of experience in academic endeavors, while George Dupey ably assisted him. Miss Doris Benner, affectionately known as "Ma" Benner, joined the staff in 1944 and held many important positions. The home at 139 North Sandusky Street was named in her honor and housed twenty-four women students for many years.

By 1956, the Remmele Building's second and third

floors were home to the college for nearly thirty-nine years. To hide the fact that the ground floor was used for retail purposes, in the early 1950s, college catalogs and promotional materials pictured the building surrounded by billowing clouds blocking out the first floor. The Remmele Building became appropriately nicknamed the "Campus in the Clouds" by alumni and friends of the era. That would soon change. Through Tiffin Mayor Robert Booth, President Pfeiffer learned that the local schools were auctioning one of their historic school buildings on the west side of town. The mayor arranged a meeting with Tiffin City Board President Leonard Gaydos, and over a July golf game an agreement was reached. The university's bid was accepted, and on December 18, 1956, students, faculty, and administrators joined to move to this new collegiate home. Thus, President Pfeiffer's greatest achievement of his twenty-eight-year presidency was to bring the college out of the clouds and place it on the ground in a more suitable campus. A historic and architecturally significant structure in a residential neighborhood, the "Main" classroom building became Tiffin University's signature structure and the center for the modern campus that would develop.

The university's campus slowly grew around the new building, led by the purchase of a dozen residential houses throughout the 1960s. One building—the former Moltry's Grocery Store—was constructed in 1872 and was purchased by the university in 1968. It later became Seitz Hall, the university's administration building. After a series of failed fund-raising efforts, the university successfully raised enough funds to construct its first building: a much-needed library. Romie J. Stahl, director of Alumni Relations during this time, should be credited with the only fund-raising success of this era.[16] The board authorized its construction on June 26, 1967, and it was dedicated Pfeiffer Library ten years later. Tiffin University averaged two hundred full-time students and graduated an average class of sixty-two throughout the 1960s. Most of the students were enrolled in the two-year program, and the Board of Trustees and President Pfeiffer feared that this trend threaten the future of the institution. But expanding the curriculum, obtaining North Central Association accreditation, and developing the physical plant seemed a daunting task.

The 1970s brought new challenges—namely, growing competition from newly formed community colleges and the need to secure proper academic accreditation, both of which compounded Tiffin University's growing financial instability and threatened the college's survival. It was obvious to many that the school had to reorganize its academic offerings. Criminal Justice was added as a major in 1970. On May 15, 1970, the Ohio Board of Regents certified that Tiffin University's two-year standard junior college course could be upgraded to an associate in Business Technology degree and reaffirmed the university's ability to offer the four-year bachelor of Commercial Science. This allowed the university to fully participate in the newly initiated federal and state financial aid programs, in turn, serving more veterans returning from the Vietnam War.

The early 1970s were characterized by low enrollments and annual operating deficits. However, the returning veterans would temporarily help. Enrollment quickly increased from 1973 until the university posted its largest enrollment to date (624) in 1976. Unfortunately, many of the returning veterans were recruited by a questionable outside firm, who enticed them with federal and state financial assistance that superseded tuition. Understandably, few in this cohort graduated. Concurrently, financial concerns and lack of terminal degrees among the faculty stopped Tiffin University from securing proper academic accreditations. Lack of residence halls forced prospective students away, and by the end of the 1978–79 academic year, 60 percent of the three hundred full-time students were enrolled in the evening program.

Pfeiffer served as president from 1953 until his retirement in 1981. He remained on the Board of Trustees until his death on July 14, 1985. Popular with students and community members, Pfeiffer maintained his accounting practice while president and enjoyed leading the college. The tools to see the institution as a modern university were absent, the entrepreneurial spirit of F. J. Miller was fading, and the 1970s were hard on Tiffin University.

A milestone occurred when George Kidd, Jr., assumed the presidency in

{George Kidd, Jr.}

April 1981. When Kidd became president, there was talk of folding the school or merging it with another institution.[17] He sought to change the perception that the university's mission was to train people to work for others. Asking stakeholders to raise their sights, Kidd set out to bring Tiffin in line with other universities. Referred to as the founder of modern Tiffin University, Kidd found a willingness in the twenty faculty and staff to change and take risks, which allowed the institution to survive long enough to become part of the fabric of higher education in Ohio. Kidd quickly launched the most explosive growth in the institution's 122-year history. He, like Miller, brought with him an able partner in his quest to save the struggling institution, Dr. John Millar. Kidd's friend and colleague played an important role in securing enrollment and academic growth. Also, Kidd's wife, Diane, an artist and graphic designer for all university publications, including the alumni and friend magazine, *Challenge*, made it a true partnership. Together, by upgrading outreach through gracious entertaining, Diane was the founder and longtime director of the university's and the area's first art gallery, which was named in her honor. Most importantly, Kidd sought to broaden educational opportunity rather than limit it. He was proud that Tiffin served students of all ages and backgrounds and believed that, if properly motivated, a college degree was in reach of most students. President Kidd's twenty-one-year tenure can be characterized as transforming a small financially troubled business school into a comprehensive university. The transformation Tiffin University experienced was remarkable.

Through a combination of new academic and co-curricular programs and physical expansion, President Kidd launched a series of five-year plans that outlined growth in every academic and non-academic area. The university received the long-sought accreditation by the North Central Association of Colleges and Schools in 1983, recognizing President Kidd's ability to attract faculty to teach in baccalaureate-level programs. In 1980, no member of the faculty held a terminal degree, and the majority of students were in the two-year programs. By 2000, 80 percent of the faculty held terminal degrees, and only 6 percent of the students were enrolled in the two-year programs. In 1983, the bachelor of Commercial Science was changed to a bachelor of Business Administration. At the same time, the university began broadening their academic offerings, which eventually resulted in the addition of the bachelor of Criminal Justice and bachelor of Arts degrees. In the 1990s, Tiffin University added its first graduate degree programs. The first master of Business Administration (MBA) class graduated in 1992, and a master of Criminal Justice (MCJ) was added in 1996.

Kidd quickly changed the governance structure of the university; he expanded the seven-member Board of Trustees that met rarely and still reflected a proprietary culture that was abandoned more than fifty years earlier. Assisted by strong chairmen—Gordon Wagner, George Wollenslegel, and Gary Heminger—the board was enlarged to twenty-four members and instituted an effective committee system and met regularly, ensuring traditional oversight and fiduciary authority.

Past problems centered on not having a significant culture of philanthropy needed to properly sustain an independent school of higher learning. The culture was stuck between a for-profit commercial college and a modern university. The university was raising less than one thousand dollars a year annually and did not have a contemporary development program. President Kidd set out to change this. He added a giving club structure, professionalized the advancement efforts, and cultivated alumni and the community and asked for support.

Early philanthropic endorsements were important, maybe even critical, to Kidd's early success. Wayne Zahn, then president of National Machinery in Tiffin, and his alumnae wife, Virginia, started a successful competitive scholarship and funded a new residence hall. They were particularly helpful in jump-starting Kidd's advancement goals. Brothers Rolland and Ellsworth Friedley provided early needed support. Ellsworth credited his success as a medical doctor to his and his brother's success in business. A 1937 visit to the Friedleys' parent's farm in New Washington by then-president Franklin Miller convinced them that the fifty-dollar-a-month tuition was worth it for Rolland and the family. It was. Rolland used his acquired business skills to own a bank and an insurance agency, supporting his brother through

Miami Street School

In 1956, when Tiffin University moved to Miami Street, it came to rest in a largely Italian-American neighborhood. Industrial concerns shared the neighborhood with the Miami Street School and a variety of shops that served the immigrants. The future campus would be framed by the railroad to the north, a scrapyard to the west, and St. Mary's Church to the east.

The land that the Miami Street School occupied was first owned by Josiah Hedges and sold to the Board of Education of Tiffin by Catherine Delany on March 1, 1884, for $2,200 to build an elementary school to serve the west side of Tiffin. It was called the Third Ward School, and the Second District School at times, before it was commonly referred to the Miami Street School.

The Miami Street School was built and designed by William H. Hollenberger in a Gothic Revival style and completed in 1884 during a building boom in Tiffin. Its steeped gables, bold details, and strong vertical lines were a harbinger of the Collegiate Gothic movement that would later define collegiate architecture in the United States.

As new schools were built in the 1950s, the Miami Street School and the College Hill School to the east were displaced. Tiffin University purchased the abandoned school on September 28, 1956, for $12,200 from the board, only $10,000 more than the board paid for the land seventy-two years earlier. This purchase of a historic building set in motion a modern campus. It is called Main or the Main Classroom Building today and is listed on the National Register of Historic Places.[18]

Miami St. School, Tiffin, Ohio

Capital University and medical school. They, in turn, paid back the university in significant ways: Friedley Hall and the Bridgewater House are just two of their major contributions. The Zahns and the Friedleys—as well as Hazel Franks, P. M. and Lucy Gillmor, and Margaret Patterson Huggins—provided needed and timely backing and credibility to the new vision of a modern Tiffin University. Also during this time, the university began to attract significant foundation support, namely from the National Machinery and Meshech Frost Foundations. Don and Dorothy Bero were particularly helpful during these early times.

Town-gown relations quickly improved, helped by the advent of a breakfast lecture series, *Good Morning World*, which today is in its twenty-seventh year. Kidd's first campaign raised more than two hundred thousand dollars, which provided badly needed renovations for Seitz Hall and the Main Classroom Building, the future historic anchors of a new campus vision. With the help of Goettler Associates of Columbus, three successful capital campaigns—*The Tiffin University Challenge Campaign* (1987–1988) during the centennial, *The Campaign for Tiffin University* (1994–1996), and *Invest in What Matters, A Campaign for Tiffin University* (2000–2003)—changed the culture of giving in less than twenty years. In 1999, Tiffin University was awarded the Circle of Excellence Award for Educational Fund Raising for Overall Improvement from the Council for the Advancement and Support of Education (CASE). In 1995, the university turned a generous gift from Robert and Eugenie Friedman into Freidman Village, an independent and assisted living campus along St. Francis Avenue that the school operated for more than fourteen years before selling it to St. Francis Ministries.

The way Tiffin University was viewed as an institution of higher learning was changing as it approached its centennial. Conscious actions were taken to break from the singular culture of a business school for training purposes. In honor of the one hundredth anniversary, the university seal was modified and the motto was changed. The old seal had the words, *Schola Commerci*, roughly meaning *School of Commerce*. The new, crisper seal now donned the words *Sine Audacia Nullum Praemium*, translated as *without risk, there is no gain.* Both the seal and the motto were adopted by the Board of Trustees in February 1987. Nine years later, Shane O'Donnell wrote and composed and Brad Rees arranged a new *Alma Mater* as well as the first-ever fight song. Their inaugural introduction took place at *The Campaign for Tiffin University* victory party in 1996. Coach Bob Wolfe's 1996 football team was the first to sing the fight song.

{Left: Construction site of Gillmor Student Center}

{Below: Benner Hall was located at 139 North Sandusky Street.}

Word of mouth about the changes at Tiffin University became the best recruiter. Students began enrolling from beyond the traditional fifty-mile radius. Enrollment skyrocketed. Many needed a place to live. The three-acre campus of 1980 expanded to eleven acres in 1990 and to more than 130 acres in 2000. President Kidd led an effort to develop a total residential student experience, adding professional student personnel and residence halls. He constructed seven residence halls in a sixteen-year span, including Veard Hall (later named Friedley) (1984), Zahn (1985), Miller (1992), Craycraft (1990), Huggins (1994), Kirk (2000), and Benner (2000). As a part of the centennial celebration, the Gillmor Student Center was dedicated in 1988, the largest construction project to date, in honor of Paul and Lucy Gillmor, longtime benefactors of Tiffin University. Housing a gymnasium as well as a complement of student service amenities, its size doubled in 2001 when it was expanded to include a theatre and new dining hall. The four intercollegiate athletic teams in 1980 quickly expanded to sixteen, including football in 1985. Tiffin University was accepted in the National Collegiate Association of Athletics (NCAA) in 1999 and now competes at the Division II level. The Hanson Clutch Factory was added to the campus and became widely used as a fitness center and maintenance building. Later, Margaret Hanson Reed would leave the university a significant endowment. In 1992, the university added seventy-eight acres of modern athletic fields and locker rooms.

As Tiffin University entered the last decade of the twentieth century, the vision of a unified campus became a reality. The Legacy Courtyard joined together the north campus along Miami Street in 1991, as enrollment, for the first time, surpassed one thousand. It was made possible largely by the philanthropy of Hazel Craycraft Franks, whose two new buildings, Craycraft Hall, a resident hall, and Franks Hall, an academic building, nicely frame the north campus. After a series of land purchases and street and alley vacations, the eleven acres that was once home to more than thirty houses, buildings, and shops, six alleys, and two streets was transformed into an attractive campus. A similar conversion took place on the south side of Miami Street where fourteen houses and three alley vacations made way for three new residence halls.[19]

The academic transformation mirrored the physical growth. The university grew into its name, realizing the dreams of F. J. Miller and A. M. Reichard, by reorganizing its academic divisions into schools. In 1996, Tiffin University divided into the School of Business, the School of Arts and Sciences, the School of Criminal Justice, and a Graduate School. At the turn of the century, Tiffin University enrolled sixteen hundred undergraduate and graduate students at its main campus in Tiffin, online, at the University of Bucharest in Romania, and at several other locations in Ohio. Tiffin University is truly a comprehensive university.

Dr. George Kidd, Jr., announced his retirement in 2001 after twenty-one years of transformational leadership. On July 1, 2002, Dr. Paul B. Marion became the fourth president of Tiffin University. The former president of Franklin College in Indiana, Dr. Marion came to Tiffin University with thirty-four years of successful experience in higher education, including seventeen years as a chief executive officer. Tiffin University under his leadership quickly rose to approximately two thousand students in undergraduate and graduate degree programs by 2006.

President Marion quickly seized the legacies of the past, positioning the college for the next century as a nimble, entrepreneurial institution able to recognize and capitalize on the new educational landscape of the day. His wife, Susan, also added greatly to the life of the college: counseling students, contributing to campus beautification, and assisting with the music program. They were the first family to occupy the Schriner House, a twenty-four-acre estate donated to the university by the late Dr. Robert and Mary Schriner to serve as the official presidential residence. President Marion said Tiffin University is a new kind of university, a professional university, a place of access and opportunity, where the American Dream is manifested:

Tiffin University is neither a liberal arts college, a research university, nor a "virtual" university. It's a hybrid with a distinctive strategy and approach. We don't try to be all things to all people—but what we choose to do, we do well.

Marion's entrepreneurial management style proved to be successful, as shown by the university's growth in physical and academic measures. TU takes advantage of its entrepreneurial spirit by continuing to pursue partnerships that aid the university in growth and financial stability. For example, teacher education programs are offered through a partnership with Lourdes College in Toledo. The first decade of the twenty-first century is marked by a trajectory of steady growth. The enrollment has more than doubled, reaching 2,357 students in 2007 and 3,429 in 2009. Full-time faculty increased by 86 percent, reducing class sizes substantially. Fifteen new undergraduate majors, many in the liberal arts, were established.

{Paul Marion}

Also thirty-two academic minors and an honors program were instituted. Tiffin gained membership in the Great Lakes Intercollegiate Athletic Conference (GLIAC) in 2008 and added a competitive equestrian program, women's lacrosse, and wrestling. Tiffin University promotes a life of learning for its constituents in many ways: It provides a relevant, practical curriculum, offers its programs in multiple modalities and locations, and remains abreast of cultural and global trends. The Tiffin campus is home to fourteen hundred residential students, and the school's online network is extensive. Online, Tiffin serves as an educational headquarters to several locations in Ohio, including Columbus, Cleveland, Elyria, Toledo, and Fremont. In addition, Tiffin has a presence in four foreign countries. Master's degrees are offered in Bucharest and Timisoara, Romania; Taipei, Taiwan; Prague, Czech Republic; and Warsaw and Pozner, Poland. More than fifteen hundred students seek a Tiffin University degree online each year. A master of Education and master of Humanities are the most recent additions to Tiffin's graduate program.[20]

What Matters

The largest and most comprehensive campaign in the university's history was completed in 2003. *Invest in What Matters* raised more than $11.2 million allowing, among other additions, the construction of two new buildings. The

{Possibly the largest and most comprehensive urban renewal project in the history of Tiffin, a $30 million investment turned this former ten-acre brownfield into a Living Learning Community, built by UHS, along with a new 122,000 square-foot recreation center. Funds from *Share the Pride. Build on Tradition. A Campaign for Tiffin University* joined city, state, and federal agencies in making this possible. Senator Sherrod Brown was particularly helpful in this transformation.}

Hayes Center for the Arts, which includes a professional-quality art gallery, art studios, music rehearsal rooms, and a chapel, was built in honor of David and Patty Hayes. The Hertzer Technology Center was made possible by William and Jean Hertzer, in memory of their son William Jr. Twenty-nine buildings—all but five built since 1985—span more than 130 acres.

On November 15, 2006, the Tiffin University athletic facility was given a new name. The former Bell farm, transformed over a ten-year period into a premier Division II outdoor facility, became the Paradiso Athletic Complex. It now houses Heminger Baseball Field, varsity softball, soccer, outdoor track and field, practice areas for football, and locker rooms. Tiffin University carved out twenty-nine acres of deep, streamside forest within the complex to create the Tiffin University Nature Preserve through a partnership with the state of Ohio and the Seneca County Park District. It was dedicated on June 5, 2007. A mile-long nature trail winds through a forested floodplain wetlands and vernal pools. The nature preserve provides an enhanced natural setting for gatherings of students and staff, as well as accessible natural areas for Tiffin and Seneca County–area citizens.

In 2006, President Marion led the largest building project in the university's history, and possibly the largest urban renewal project in the city's annals. It began with the bold acquisition of the ten-acre site formerly occupied by the Rosenblatt Scrap Yard, which bisects Miami Street just west of the campus. For more than fifty years, this ten-acre, polluted scrap yard bordered the campus. Complex environmental and relationship issues clouded a resolution; many accepted the situation, few saw a solution. Federal, state, and local agencies joined the university and its philanthropic friends in turning this Tiffin eyesore into a restored brown-field, which allowed for a more than $30 million renaissance along this new Miami Street corridor. The south side is anchored by a $17 million Living-Learning Community made possible by philanthropist/developer Dr. Frank Murphy and University Housing Solutions. These new apartments are now a home for 244 students, and the complex includes four classrooms. On the north rises the largest collegiate building in Tiffin, a new 122,000-square-foot indoor recreation center, replete with two connecting buildings: one large enough to house an NCAA regulation indoor track and the other a field house home to sixty yards of field turf. This was coupled with the Miami Street Improvement Project—decorative street enhancements along our main corridor made possible by the late congressman Paul Gillmor, which serves a fitting ending to our saga.

Tiffin University now has a large footprint with the wider Tiffin, Ohio, community, its surrounding region, and increasingly on a global level. The students of Tiffin University are diverse in terms of age, educational background, race and ethnicity, and mode of educational delivery.[21]

In 2010, the Higher Learning Commission (HLC)—North Central Association of Colleges and Schools—re-accredited Tiffin University for another ten years.

In doing so the visiting team was very positive and endorsed the university as a place of access and opportunity:

TU has responded to the need of upgrading its facilities in a way that makes the traditional campus program more appealing to the typical college-age student and has positioned itself as not only a place to earn a quality education but boasts of an attractive setting in which to do so.

TU should be applauded for its efforts it has made to keep tuition affordable and to offer the chance to a sometimes overlooked demographic among college hopefuls. TU has re-tooled several of its student services to assist the many first generation students that choose to enroll.

Tiffin University, as it nears its 125th anniversary, is now lauded as the fastest growing higher education institution in Ohio. TU has a total enrollment for fall 2010 of 4,940 students from all fifty states and thirty countries, and others have taken notice. According to C. Todd Jones, president of the Association of Independent Colleges and Universities of Ohio, "Tiffin University's headcount enrollment grew by 128 percent from the fall of 2003 to the fall of 2009, which made Tiffin the fastest growing college or university in Ohio during that period." Dr. DeBow Freed, lauded president emeritus of both Ohio Northern University and the University of Findlay, adds

Tiffin University stands among the top few institutions in the country in the extent and consistency of improving its programs, facilities, and standing among colleges and universities on a national basis. Its progressive upward movement in all phases of its operations and University life has truly been remarkable.

Tiffin University is in the midst of a remarkable academic and physical transformation. The effort has been underway for the last several decades, and the growth has been guided by keen vision and an entrepreneurial spirit. The success can be credited to committed trustees, strong administrative leadership, engaged faculty and staff, and dedicated alumni, donors, and parents who join together daily to deliver knowledge and commitment to the students.

End Notes

1   *Tiffin Advertiser-Tribune*, January 26, 1938.

2   Stock certificate book.

3   Miller tried often to find a way to trade the farm for his stake in the company. Federal tax laws and Ohio corporate laws repeatedly blocked him. A legal opinion by an attorney is outlined in a letter between Miller and Attorney Martin, dated October 11, 1945.

4   Family history of the McNeal's, a letter from Fran Fleet.

5   W. Lang. *History of Seneca County, from the Close of the Revolutionary War to July 1880.* Springfield, Ohio: Transcript Printing Company, 1880, 312.

6   Tiffin Tribune, April 18, 1872.

7   Tiffin Business University Board of Trustees Minutes, November 10, 1939.

8   Tiffin Business University Board of Trustees Minutes, October 15, 1942.

9   Inflation Calculator: http://www.westegg.com/inflation/infl.cgi.

10 Tiffin Business University Board of Trustees Minutes, February 1, 1945.

11 Tiffin Business University Board of Trustees Minutes, May 2, 1952.

12 Tiffin Business University Board of Trustees Minutes, May 14, 1948.

13 Tiffin Business University Board of Trustees Minutes, January 22, 1951. Between the Internal Revenue Service, local lawyers, and steadfast trustees, Tiffin University survived a struggle to wrestle with how to become truly non-profit. Quite understandably, everyone wanted their money: $290,000 in today's dollars was owed. Some sacrifices were made; some back-room deals were probably struck. From any prospective, Tiffin University would have unlikely survived as a for-profit institution with Miller and Reichard at the twilight of their careers. This act truly institutionalized Tiffin University.

14 Tiffin Business University Board of Trustees Minutes, February 5, 1948.

15 Personal interview with F. J. Miller's daughter Margaret Swineburne. Albuquerque, N.M., 2003.

16 Romie J. Stahl Letter Collection, Tiffin University Archives, 1964–65.

17 Personal communication with Thomas O. Giebel.

18 Survey and transaction work at the Seneca County's Recorder's Office by Barry Porter.

19 Sanborn Fire Insurance Maps: 1867–1970. www.Ohiolink.edu.

20 Institutional Snapshot, NCA Accreditation Study, 2010.

21 Self Study Report for the Higher Learning Commission, North Central Association of Colleges and School, 2010.

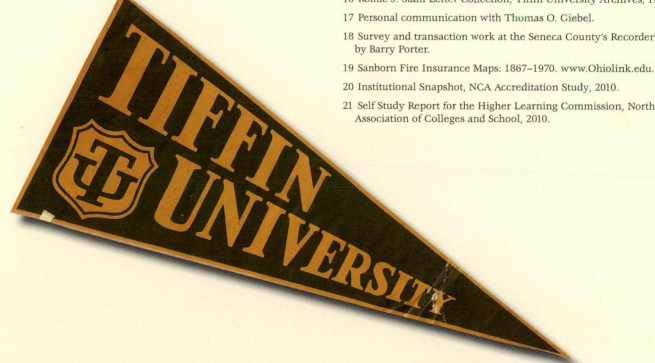

Epilogue

Onward to the Dawn

On Friday, September 16, 1988, at approximately 11:00 a.m., President George Kidd convened the Centennial Convocation of Tiffin University at the new Gillmor Student Center. Although all one hundred-year anniversaries are replete with history, this celebration went beyond the long line of delegates of sister institutions and public officials; it brought the newly emerging collegiate force full circle. Following the convocation address by Dr. James Fisher, a noted leader and author on effective college presidential leadership, President Kidd conferred an honorary degree posthumously upon George Williard. The man whose ideal was the seed that created the modern Tiffin University was now an alumnus. Robert Williard accepted the honor on behalf of his great-grandfather. Robert presented the university with a portrait of the extolled Heidelberg president. His visage now hangs in the Heritage Room alongside ensuing presidents.[1]

Everyone gathered that day was not as concerned about past history as how much they were a part of the history of Tiffin University. Faculty and staff believed a successful academic infrastructure and campus was being built. The Gillmors and the Zahns gave the university needed and timely philanthropic boosts; and the completion of the new Gillmor Center helped even the most discerning stakeholders see that risks can make gains. Third Ward Councilman Joseph H. Granata—who worked with the city of Tiffin to shepherd more than seven street and alley vacations that cleared the way for buildings, green space, and the legacy courtyard that now spans from the entire north side of Miami Street—was looking on from the assembly with delight that day. A sense a permanence permeated the day. For many, this was a turning point.[2] Was this the dawn? Fisher may have summed it up in his address that day:

One should not be surprised that the public perception on Tiffin University is generally excellent. The image of the university has clearly changed from a good but rather parochial institution to an important and exciting presence in this region and beyond.[3]

A Historical Analysis—The First Fifty Years

The late nineteenth century was a period of exceptional dynamic economic expansion and accompanying social change. This was particularly true in the newly settled agricultural lands on the western edge of the nation. The development of new and improved modes of transportation linking West and East fueled rapid population growth and a culture that valued expansion, enterprise, and risk-taking. An accelerating introduction of innovative mechanical devises and labor-saving tools strengthened this entrepreneurial drive and increased economic opportunities. Ohio was at the forefront of this movement, and the rural towns of the state, originally struggling agricultural settlements, saw exponential growth and transformation into multifaceted commercial and industrial communities.

No traditional institutions escape the effect of these changes. Higher education in particular was influenced by the need to provide the ever-expanding range of practical skills necessary for the growth of such communities and employment of their citizens. The same spirit of boosterism that brought railways and bridges to rural Ohio also led to the expansion of educational opportunity. The old apprentice system of professional training gave way to courses of study, first alongside traditional, or classical, colleges and then incorporated with their total curricula.

The commercial college—providing instruction in bookkeeping, penmanship, and later typewriting—proved a particularly vigorous example of this pattern of growth and change. Entrepreneurs seized the opportunity for developing such institutions, encouraged by the ease of securing charters, the availability of capital, the support of local business communities, and the growing market for services. Tiffin, Ohio, as a prototypical example of such a community, proved a fertile ground for the development of such varied educational institutions after the Civil War and supported a number of commercial colleges.

While an approach to education that emphasizes an adherence to enduring and unchanging cultural knowledge and traditional values has been a constant in American life, educational philosophies and practices have been highly responsive to economic and social change. Education has never been successful isolated from the contexts of everyday practical life. Never was this more evident than in the development of commercial education in the rapidly changing landscape of late-nineteenth-century Ohio.

Tiffin University finds its historical foundation in the progressive vision of Heidelberg president George Williard when he founded a commercial college as an independent department in 1888. A progressive college president and inclusive religious leader, Williard and his governing board sought to expand Heidelberg's struggling Literary College by embracing the popular university movement of the late nineteenth century. This vision, if institutionalized, could have changed the character of Heidelberg College and expanded its outreach. A messy political fight within the Board of Regents and philosophical differences between future presidents and the Commercial College leaders did not allow this to happen. Instead, the Commercial College became more independent from Heidelberg as ownership passed from principal to principal until it landed in the hands of F. J. Miller. Miller grew the sleepy department into its own college, adding amenities, emphasizing employment of his graduates, and experimenting in international education. His success and his philosophical disagreements with Chancellor Charles Miller of Heidelberg led to a dramatic break-up, forcing each school to go their separate way.

The struggle between the Commercial College and the Literary College within the loose association of schools and programs that characterized Heidelberg University at the turn of the century exemplifies a fundamental debate within higher education at this time. Should collegiate education serve the new commercial spirit of the land, preparing students for the practical tasks of an expanding industrial economy, or should such an education serve the more traditional and conservative goal of providing immigrant communities with learned and pious religious leaders and teachers? The 1880s and 1890s saw an attempted accommodation between the two positions; a union based more on Heidelberg College's practical need for financial stability in the 1870s than on any natal alliance of the two opposing philosophies. This marriage, however, despite the best efforts of leaders like President Williard, was never institutionally consummated. The two parts of Heidelberg remained separated, eyed each other with suspicion, and competed for resources. The Commercial College, although it

brought energy, income, and numbers to the association, remained a poor relation throughout most of the period. It could not have been otherwise. The college was an upstart. In celebrating the economic dynamism of the post–Civil War years, it championed a development that was as much resisted by older members of society as it was embraced by a new generation of industrializing elites, land spectators, and merchants. The two schools represented antagonistic positions, even two different understandings of the nature of the new industrial America (as illustrated by the conflicts associated with the local Cuban experiment in international education and commercial opportunity.)

The two Millers stood at opposite poles of this clash of cultures, and their conflicting educational philosophies led to a competition for both students and status within the Tiffin community. The differences in behavior and character between the two men widened the space between them and made further collaboration impossible. Principal F. J. Miller was a flamboyant personality, a tireless self-promoter, a man of the age. Chancellor Charles Miller was an ascetic clergyman, suspicious of modern ideas, and committed to the Kingdom of Heaven rather than the earthly paradise of material success. Their parting was mutual, and the road each took significant for the future of higher education in Tiffin.

The years of 1917–1939 represent the time Tiffin University was known as Tiffin Business University. After leaving the Heidelberg University campus in

1917, F. J. Miller and A. M. Reichard incorporated their for-profit educational enterprise and began to dramatically alter higher education in Tiffin. Together, they made progressive, calculated, educational business decisions that built a university and made them financially comfortable. This time also gives us insight into the peculiarly American institution: the for-profit proprietary college. We learn how it was funded, incorporated, and governed. We learn how it depended on its customers.

Franklin Miller was both an altruistic soul and a shrewd businessman. His financial dealings and his management of the university clearly demonstrate both characteristics. His move to non-profit status was based in both his personal desire to recoup his investment and his desire to perpetuate commercial education in Tiffin for poor men and women of good character.

Whatever constituted his motives, his actions worked. In ten short years, he transformed a sleepy commercial college into a junior college and more. He shaped and molded its curriculum and extracurricular offerings for success. Tiffin Business University boldly grew from offering diplomas to bachelor's degrees. The lobbying efforts of Miller with the state of Ohio, his attempt to create his own associations to lend the aura of membership and credentialing, his extending of athletics, and other outside activities were important advancements. He was an extraordinary leader, and he created the illusion of a more substantial institution than was the case.

Miller and Reichard were truly remarkable educational entrepreneurs who used the city of Tiffin as their campus. The relocation to, and investment in, a modern downtown building was a forward-looking move and demonstrates the importance of myriad physical structures that support the programs of a higher education institution. F. J. Miller's formula of aggressive advertising, quality instruction, and unrelenting job placement made Tiffin Business University, and Miller, financially successful. Success permitted Miller to be more aggressive in pontificating his educational philosophy to a wider public.

Most importantly, Tiffin Business University serves as an excellent example of the adjustments made in higher education in the early twentieth century. TBU thrived in the 1920s and brilliantly survived the Depression of the 1930s due to its ability to provide a more practical and job-oriented education. Miller's comment about the fact that his graduates faired better in the job market than a Greek scholar—the product of a less practical education—provides keen insight into this period of higher education. The Depression gave Miller the opportunity to maximize the value of his employment-oriented marketing strategy. Miller's commitment to employment fit this moment in time—the right man at the right time—and his venture prospered.

An Institutional History

To many, a history of an institution of higher learning is central to the life of a college because it preserves a collective memory and interprets institutional impact on the lives of individuals and society. It brings the insights and attributes of education to life in a historical dimension. Colleges and universities are very subtle bodies. Imparting a sense of history is an important component of their existence. A collegiate history is not just a recording of classes, courses, majors, and activities; instead, it is a broad perspective on the range and scope of an institution's complete impact and involvement.

Harry Chapin ended every concert and time of sadness or celebration, such as a wedding or funeral, with the same song: *Circle*.[4] It is still sung thirty years after his death to call to mind the cyclical nature of our being, of institutional renaissance and retraction, and of the slow, but perpetual, winding clock of history.

> *All my life's a circle;*
> *Sunrise and sundown;*
> *Moon rolls thru the nighttime;*
> *Till the daybreak comes around.*

Often we do come full circle, and we do move perpetually onward to the dawn. When did the dawn arrive for Tiffin University? Was it when the idea of a commercial college was born in the mind of George Williard? Was it when Miller and Reichard separated to give the school an independent identity and purpose? Was it when for-profit Tiffin Business University became non-profit Tiffin University? Was it when Richard Pfeiffer took the campus out of the clouds and placed it physically and culturally forever on solid ground? Was it when George Kidd arrived and affected an academic and physical transformation through planning, action, and risk-taking? Or was it the recent trajectory under Paul Marion that has resulted in a meteoric rise?

History has a way of bringing us back to where we began with added enthusiasm and wisdom. Our contemporary local boosters in Tiffin celebrate with renewed vigor the benefit of having higher learning institutions in their community. Josiah Hedges would be pleased at their sagacious echoing of his harboring call. George Williard is an alumnus of Tiffin University, and Heidelberg is now a university again. And Tiffin University boldly embraces the liberal arts through its undergraduate School of Art and Sciences, art and music programs, and a graduate level master of Humanities. Maybe Mark Twain said it right: "The past may not repeat itself, but it sure does rhyme."

The dawn is that brief time between darkness and twilight. It is the act of rising, the beginning, the becoming, an advent. It is the moment of perception and understanding. Whatever the reason or cause for the daybreak, it is clear it arrived and the dawn is here and the sun now shines brightly on Tiffin University.

'Tis the place where I have grown, where my heart resides.
Green and Gold I long for you, You're my Tiffin pride.
You're my Tiffin University, You're my Tiffin home!

Every where that I shall go, there you shall be,
Leading us in life's parade, All this due to thee!
You're my Tiffin University, You're my Tiffin home!

Memories we'll keep of you as our lives move on,
While your spirit points the way, Onward to the dawn!
You're my Tiffin University, You're my Tiffin home.

—Tiffin University Alma Mater

End Notes

1   Centennial Program, September 16, 1988.

2   The author was in attendance that day in his role as 4th Ward councilman for the city of Tiffin. The sense of permanence was keenly evident.

3   *Challenge Magazine*, Fall 1988, 5.

4   *Circle*, by Harry Chapin. Several personal conversations with Harry Chapin from 1978 to 1981 and work in support of his efforts with world hunger. One particularly enjoyable visit was when Harry came to Ohio Northern University in Ada, Ohio, for a benefit concert for his World Hunger Initiative on May 7, 1981. Steve Smith assisted me with transportation and Robert Hock with photography. Mark Cook and Tom Stein also assisted. Tragically, this was one of his last concerts. Harry Chapin died on July 16, 1981, in a car crash on the Long Island Expressway.

Works Consulted

Primary Sources

Heidelberg College Archival Material

Acts and Proceeding of the Ohio Synod of the Reformed Church.

A History of the University Movement.

Aurora, Heidelberg College Yearbook, 1888–1917.

The Charter of Heidelberg University.

The Chancellorship of Heidelberg University: A Reply.

The Chancellorship of Heidelberg University: A Reply. Part Second.

Heidelberg College Board of Trustees Minutes, 1886–1890.

Heidelberg University Board of Regents Minutes, 1890–1917.

Heidelberg College Catalogue, 1888–1890.

Heidelberg University Catalogue, 1891–1917.

Kilikilik, Heidelberg College Student Newspaper, 1886–1917.

Heidelberg College Faculty Minutes, 1885–1917.

Reports of the President, Acting Chancellor, or Chancellor, 1888–1918.

Tiffin Business University Archival Material

Collection of Letters.

Incorporating Documents.

Request to Increase the Capital Stock Document.

Financial Ledger of Franklin J. Miller, Heidelberg Commercial College, 1912–1917.

Financial Ledgers of The Tiffin Business University Company.

Tiffin Business University Catalogue, 1917–1939.

The Tiffin Business University Company Stockholders Minutes, 1917–1939.

Tiffin Business University Board of Trustees Minutes, 1917–1939.

Stock Certificate Book.

Tiffin University Archival Material

Accreditation Reports, 1983, 2000, 2010.

Centennial Program, 1988.

Challenge, Magazine of Tiffin University, 1984–Present.

Tiffin University Board of Trustees Minutes, 1939–1981.

Financial Records of Tiffin University, 1917–1981.

Ledger, Tiffin University Yearbook, 1955–1981.

The Periodic Summary, Alumni Newsletter, 1955–1981.

Adrian College Archival Material

John Kost papers.

Defiance College Archival Material

Oraculum, Defiance College Yearbook, 1914.

Firsthand Accounts in Written Form

Addresses in honor of the founders of Heidelberg College Tiffin, Ohio: delivered in Rickly Chapel by Chancellor Charles E. Miller on October 2, 1930, under the auspices of Ohio Synod of the Reformed Church.

Autobiography of George W. Williard, 1900.

Letter from Attorney Martin to F.J. Miller, October 11, 1945.

Personal reminiscences of Franklin J. Miller.

Personal Letter from A. M. Reichard to Richard Pfeiffer, no date.

Reminiscing About Tiffin University, by A. M. Reichard, 1957.

The Inception of the Idea, and Incidents Leading to the Founding of Tiffin University, by F. J. Miller, 1957.

The Story of Three Dr. Williards of Tiffin and Seneca County, by Dr. N. Eugene Williard.

Family History of the McNeals by Fran Fleet.

City Directories, Census Data, Government Documents, and Other Misc. Public Records

Brookhovin Tiffin City Directory, 1901–1903.

Polk City Directory, 1892–1893.

Lawrence and Company Directory of Tiffin, Volume Two, 1915.

Northwest Territory Centennial Commission, *The Northwest Ordinance of 1787*. Washington, D.C.: U.S. Government Printing Office.

Ohio Constitution, of 1802.

Seneca County, Ohio, Deed Records, Office of the Seneca County Recorder.

The Annual Statistical Report of the Secretary of State to the Governor and the General Assembly of the State of Ohio for the Year Ending November 15, 1912, Compiled by Charles H. Graves, Secretary of State. Springfield, Ohio: The Springfield Publishing Company, State Printers, 1913.

The Annual Statistical Report of the Secretary of State to the Governor and the General Assembly of the State of Ohio for the Year Ending June 30, 1919. Compiled by Harvey C. Smith, Secretary of State. Springfield, Ohio: The Springfield Publishing Company, State Printers, 1919.

The Census of the United States of America, 1890.

The Census of the United States of America, 1930.

Wiggins Tiffin and Seneca County Directory, 1888–1890.

Newspapers

The New York Times.

Tiffin Advertiser-Tribune, 1932–2005.

Tiffin Daily Advertiser, 1888–1932.

Tiffin Seneca Advertiser, 1888–1932.

Tiffin Tribune, 1888–1933.

Tiffin Weekly Tribune, 1888–1919.

Tiffin Daily Tribune and Herald, 1887–1922.

Toledo Blade, May 3, 2009.

Artifacts

Alma Mater of Tiffin Business University.

Christmas Homecoming Dance Program, December 19, 1929.

Flyer of the North-western Normal School of Fostoria, Ohio.

Sample Ballot. Election of Tuesday, November 5, 1918.

Secondary Sources

Books on American History

Abbot, Carl. *Boosters and Businessmen: Contributions in American Studies; No. 33.* Westport, Conn.: Greenwood Press, 1981.

Appleton, D. *Appletons' Annual Cyclopedia and Register of Important Events: Embracing Political, Military, and Ecclesiastical Affairs; Public Documents; Biography, Statistics, Commerce, Finance, Literature, Science, Agriculture, and Mechanical Industry, Volume XV.* New York: D. Appleton and Company, 1890.

Boorstin, Daniel J. *The Americans: The Colonial Experience.* New York: Random House, 1958.

Boorstin, Daniel J. *The Americas: The Democratic Experience.* New York: Random House, 1973.

Boorstin, Daniel. J. *Hidden Histories: Exploring Our Secret Past.* New York: Random House, 1995.

Chernow, Ron. *Titan: The Life of John D. Rockefeller, Sr.* New York: Random House, 1998.

Cherrington, Ernst Hurst. *The Evolution of Prohibition in the United States of America: A Chronological History of the Liquor Problem and the Temperance Movement in the United States from the Earliest Settlements to the Consummation of National Prohibition.* Westerville, Ohio: The American Issue Press, 1920.

Glaab, Charles N. *Kansas City and the Railroads: Community Policy in the Growth of a Regional Metropolis.* Lawrence: University Press of Kansas, 1993.

_____. *The American City: A Documentary History.* Homewood, Ill.: Dorsey Press, 1963.

Glaab, Charles N., and Morgan Barclay. *Toledo: Gateway to the Great Lakes.* Tulsa, Okla.: Continental Heritage Press, 1982.

Glaab, Charles N., and A. Theodore Brown. *A History of Urban America.* New York: Macmillan, 1976.

Gordon, Sarah H. *Passage to Union: How the Railroad Transformed American Life.* Chicago: Ivan R. Dee, 1996.

Nevins, Allan. *Study in Power: John D. Rockefeller, Industrialist and Philanthropist.* New York: Scribners, 1953.

North, Douglas C. *Growth and Welfare in the American Past.* Englewood Cliffs, N.J.: Prentice Hall, 1996.

Stover, John F. *American Railroads.* Chicago: University of Chicago Press, 1976.

Van Riper, Paul. *History of the United States Civil Service.* Evanston, Ill.: Row, Peterson, 1958.

Willey, Malcolm MacDonald, and the American Association of University Professors, Committee Y. *Depression, Recovery and Higher Education*, 1st ed. New York: McGraw-Hill Book Company, 1937.

Books on Higher Education

Adams, Charles Kendall. *Washington and the Higher Education; an Address Delivered before Cornell University, February 22, 1888.* Ithaca, N.Y.: Andrus & Church, 1888.

Altman, Robert A. *The Upper Division College.* San Francisco: Jossey-Bass, 1970.

Astin, Alexander W., Calvin B. T. Lee, and Carnegie Commission on Higher Education. *The Invisible Colleges: A Profile of Small, Private Colleges with Limited Resources.* New York: McGraw-Hill, 1971.

Beach, Mark. *A Subject Bibliography of the History of American Higher Education.* Westport, Conn.: Greenwood Press, 1984.

Birnbaum, Robert. "Value of Different Kinds of Colleges," in *Foundations of American Higher Education: An ASHE Reader, ASHE Reader Series*, edited by James L. Bess and Association for the Study of Higher Education. Needham Heights, Mass.: Ginn Press, 1991.

Blackmar, Frank W. *The History of Federal and State Aid to Higher Education in the United States.* Washington, D.C.: Government Printing Office, 1890.

Blandin, Isabella Margaret Elizabeth. *History of Higher Education of Women in the South Prior to 1860.* New York: The Neale Publishing Company, 1909.

Bledstein, Burton J. *The Culture of Professionalism: The Middle Class and the Development of Higher Education in America.* New York: Norton, 1976.

Bowles, Frank Hamilton, Frank A. DeCosta, and Carnegie Commission on Higher Education. *Between Two Worlds: A Profile of Negro Higher Education.* New York: McGraw-Hill, 1971.

Brickman, William W., and Stanley Lehrer. *A Century of Higher Education: Classical Citadel to Collegiate Colossus.* Westport, Conn.: Greenwood Press, 1974.

Brubacher, John Seiler, and Willis Rudy. *Higher Education in Transition: A History of American Colleges and Universities, 1636–1968.* New York: Harper & Row, 1968.

Casper, Dale E. *Recent Writings on the History of American Higher Education, Published 1974–1981, Public Administration Series--Bibliography, P-1226.* Monticello, Ill.: Vance Bibliographies, 1983.

Conn, Robert, and Michael Nickerson. *United Methodists and Their Colleges: Themes in the*

History of a College-Related Church. Nashville, Tenn.: United Methodist Board of Higher Education and Ministry, 1989.

Cremin, Lawrence Arthur. *American Education: The Metropolitan Experience, 1876–1980*. New York: Harper & Row, 1988.

_____. *American Education: The National Experience, 1783–1876*. New York: Harper & Row, 1980.

_____. *American Education: The Colonial Experience, 1607–1783*. New York: Harper & Row, 1970.

Cubberley. Ellwood P. *History of Education: Educational Practice and Progress Considered as a Phase of the Development and Spread of Western Civilization*. Boston: Houghton Mifflin. 1920.

Ebersole, Mark C. *Hail to Thee, Okoboji U! A Humor Anthology on Higher Education*. New York: Fordham University Press, 1992.

Earnest, Earnest P. *Academic Procession: An Informal History of the American College, 1636 to 1953*. Indianapolis: Bobbs-Merrill, 1953.

Deighton, Lee C. *The Encyclopedia of Education*. New York: MacMillian, 1971.

Franks, Ray. *What's in a Nickname?: Exploring the Jungle of College Athletic Mascots*. Amarillo, Tex.: R. Franks Publications Ranch. 1982.

Geiger, Roger L. *The American College in the Nineteenth Century: Vanderbilt Issues in Higher Education*. Nashville: Vanderbilt University Press, 2000.

_____. *Research & Relevant Knowledge: American Research Universities since World War II, Transaction Series in Higher Education*. New Brunswick, N.J.: Transaction Publishers, 2004.

_____. *To Advance Knowledge: The Growth of American Research Universities, 1900–1940, Transaction Series in Higher Education*. New Brunswick, N.J.: Transaction Publishers, 2004.

Oleson, Sandra, and John Voss. *The Organization of Knowledge in America, 1860–1920*. Baltimore: Johns Hopkins University Press, 1978.

Goodchild, Lester F., Harold S. Wechsler, and Association for the Study of Higher Education. *ASHE Reader on the History of Higher Education, ASHE Reader Series*. Needham Heights, Mass.: Ginn Press, 1989.

Gordon, Lynn D. *Gender and Higher Education in the Progressive Era*. New Haven, Conn.: Yale University Press, 1990.

Hackensmith, Charles William. *Ohio Valley Higher Education in the Nineteenth Century*. Lexington: College of Education, University of Kentucky, 1973.

Harding, Thomas Spencer. *College Literary Societies: Their Contribution to Higher Education in the United States, 1815–1876*. New York: Pageant Press International, 1971.

Haskins, Charles Homer. *The Rise of Universities, Foundations of Higher Education*. New Brunswick, N.J.: Transaction Publishers, 2002.

Henry, David Dodds, and Carnegie Council on Policy Studies in Higher Education. *Challenges Past, Challenges Present: An Analysis of American Higher Education since 1930*. San Francisco: Jossey-Bass Publishers, 1975.

Hill, Susan, and National Center for Education Statistics. *The Traditionally Black Institutions of Higher Education, 1860 to 1982*. Washington, D.C.: U.S. Dept. of Education, Office of Educational Research and Improvement, National Center for Education Statistics, 1985.

Hines, Neal O. *Business Officers in Higher Education: A History of NACUBO*. Washington, D.C.: National Association of College and University Business Officers, 1982.

Hinton, David B. *Celluloid Ivy: Higher Education in the Movies, 1960–1990*. Metuchen, N.J.: Scarecrow Press, 1994.

Hofstadter, Richard. *Academic Freedom in the Age of the College*. New York: Columbia University Press, 1961.

Hofstadter, Richard, C. De Witt Hardy, and Commission on Financing Higher Education. *The Development and Scope of Higher Education in the United States*. New York: Columbia University Press, for the Commission on Financing Higher Education, 1952.

Hofstadter, Richard, and Walter P. Metzger. *The Development of Academic Freedom in the United States*. New York: Columbia University Press, 1955.

Hofstadter, Richard, and Wilson Smith. *American Higher Education: A Documentary History*. Chicago: University of Chicago Press, 1961.

Jenkins, Mark T. *Nickname Mania: The Best college Nicknames and Mascots and the Stories Behind Them*. Conway, Ark.: Admark Communications, 1996.

Kerr, Clark. *The Great Transformation in Higher Education, 1960–1980, SUNY Series, Frontiers in Education*. Albany: State University of New York Press, 1991.

Kerr, Clark, Marian L. Gade, and Maureen Kawaoka. *Higher Education Cannot Escape History: Issues for the Twenty-First Century, SUNY Series, Frontiers in Education*. Albany: State University of New York Press, 1994.

Koos, Leonard Vincent. *The Junior College*. Minneapolis: University of Minnesota, 1924.

Layton, Elizabeth. *Significant Dates in the Early History of Institutions for the Higher Education of Women in the United States*. Washington, D.C.: Federal Security Agency, Office of Education, Division of Higher Education, 1948.

Leslie, William L. *Gentlemen and Scholars: College and Community in the Age of the University, 1865–1917*. College Park: The Pennsylvania State University Press, 1992.

Lucas, Christopher J. *American Higher Education: A History*. 1st St. Martin's Griffin ed. New York: St. Martin's Griffin, 1996.

Monroe, Paul. *A Cyclopedia of Education, Vol. 2*. New York: The Macmillan Company, 1911.

Nord, Warren A. *Religion and American Rethinking Education: Rethinking a National Dilemma*. Chapel Hill: The University of North Carolina Press, 1995.

Ott, Steven J. *The Nature of the Nonprofit Sector*. Boulder, Colo.: Westview Press, 2001.

Portman, David N. *Early Reform in American Higher Education*. Chicago: Nelson-Hall Co., 1972.

Power, Edward J. *A History of Catholic Higher Education in the United States*. Milwaukee: Bruce Publishing Company, 1958.

Rainsford, George N. *Congress and Higher Education in the Nineteenth Century*. Knoxville: University of Tennessee Press, 1972.

Rudolph, Frederick. *The American College and University: A History*. New York: Knopf, 1962.

Rudolph, Frederick, and Carnegie Council on Policy Studies in Higher Education. *Curriculum: A History of the American Undergraduate Course of Study since 1636*. San Francisco: Jossey-Bass Publishers, 1977.

Rudolph, Frederick, and John R. Thelin. *The American College and University: A History*. Athens: University of Georgia Press, 1990.

Tewksbury, Donald George. *The Founding of American Colleges and Universities before the Civil War, with Particular Reference to the Religious Influences Bearing Upon the College Movement*. Hamden, Conn.: Archon Books, 1965.

Thelin, John R. *Higher Education and Its Useful Past: Applied History in Research and Planning*. Cambridge, Mass.: Schenkman Publishing Company, 1982.

_____. *A History of American Higher Education*. Baltimore: Johns Hopkins University Press, 2004.

Thwing, Charles F. *A History of Higher Education in America*. New York: D. Appleton and Company, 1906.

Veysey, Laurence R. *The Emergence of the American University*. Chicago: University of Chicago Press, 1965.

Westmeyer, Paul. *A History of American Higher Education*. Springfield, Ill.: Thomas, 1985.

_____. *An Analytical History of American Higher Education*. 2d ed. Springfield, Ill.: Thomas, 1997.

Whitehead, John S. *The Separation of College and State: Columbia, Dartmouth, Harvard, and Yale, 1776–1876*. New Haven, Conn.: Yale University Press, 1973

Williams, Louis L., and Fernando E. Rogers. *The New Theoretical and Practical Complete Book-Keeping by Double and Single Entry for Use in Business Colleges, Common Schools, High Schools and Academies, Williams & Rogers Series*. New York: American Book Company, 1890.

Wills, Elbert Vaughan. *The Growth of American Higher Education, Liberal, Professional and Technical*. Philadelphia: Dorrance & Company, 1936.

Books on Tiffin, Ohio, Seneca County, Northwest Ohio and the State of Ohio

Baughman, A. J. *History of Seneca County, Ohio: A Narrative Account of Its Historical Progress, Its People, and Its Principal Interests*. New York: Lewis Publishing Company, 1911.

Beauregard, Erving E. *History of Academic Freedom in Ohio: Case Studies in Higher Education, 1808–1976, American University Studies. Series IX, History; Vol. 14*. New York: P. Lang, 1988.

Bossing, Nelson L. *The History of Educational Legislation in Ohio from 1851 to 1925*. Columbus, Ohio: F.J. Heer, 1931.

Butterfield, Consul W. *History of Seneca County Ohio*. Sandusky, Ohio: D. Campbell & Sons, 1848.

Galbreath, Charles Burleigh. *History of Ohio*. Chicago: The American Historical Society, Inc., 1925.

_____. *The Story of Ohio*. Chicago: F. A. Owen Publishing Company, 1913.

Huntington, Charles C. *History of the Ohio Canals: Their Construction, Cost, Use and Partial Abandonment*. Columbus: Ohio State Archaeological and Historical Society, 1905.

Knepper, George W. *Ohio and Its People*. Kent, Ohio: Kent State University Press, 1997.

Knight, George W., and John Rogers Commons. *The History of Higher Education in Ohio*. Washington, D.C.: Government Printing Office, 1891.

Hodges, James A., James H. O'Donnell, and John W. Oliver. *Cradles of Conscience: Ohio's Independent Colleges and Universities*. Kent, Ohio: Kent State University Press, 2003.

Lang, W. *History of Seneca County, from the Close of the Revolutionary War to July 1880*. Springfield, Ohio: Transcript Printing Company, 1880.

Leeson, M. A. *History of Seneca County, Ohio*. Chicago: Warner, Beers & Company, 1886.

Souvenir Program Commemorating the Seventy-Fifth Anniversary of the Founding of the City of Tiffin, 1822–1897. Akron, Ohio: The Werner Company, 1897.

Roseboom, Eugene H. *The History of the State of Ohio*. Columbus: The Ohio State Archaeological and Historical Society, 1944.

Wittke, Carl Frederick, Beverley W. Bond, William Thomas Utter, Francis P. Weisenburger, Eugene Holloway Roseboom, Philip D. Jordan, and Harlow Lindley. *The History of the State of Ohio*. Columbus: Ohio State Archaeological and Historical Society, 1941.

Institutional Histories of Colleges and Universities

Adams, Herbert Baxter. *The College of William and Mary: A Contribution to the History of Higher Education, with Suggestions for Its National Promotion*. Washington, D.C.: Government Printing Office, 1887.

Becker, Carl. L. *Cornell University: Founders and the Founding*. Ithaca, N.Y.: Cornell University Press, 1943.

Bush, Perry. *Dancing with the Kobzar: Bluffton College and Mennonite Higher Education, 1899–1999*, Newton, Kan.: Pandora Press, 2000.

Cargo, Ruth E., Harlan L. Feeman, and Fanny A. Hay. *The Story of a Noble Devotion, 1845–1945: One Hundred Years*. Adrian, Mich.: Adrian College Press, 1945.

Carr, Howard Ernest. *Washington College; a Study of an Attempt to Provide Higher Education in Eastern Tennessee*. Knoxville, Tenn.: S.B. Newman & Co., 1935.

Cope, Alexis. *History of The Ohio State University*. Columbus: The Ohio State University Press, 1920.

Cramer, Clarence. H. *Case Western Reserve: A History of the University, 1826–1976*. Boston: Little Brown, 1976.

Edmonds, Anthony O., and E. Bruce Geelhoed. *Ball State University: An Interpretive History*. Bloomington: Indiana University Press, 2001.

Faragher, John Mack, Florence Howe, and Mount Holyoke College. *Women and Higher Education in American History: Essays from the Mount Holyoke College Sesquicentennial Symposia*. New York: Norton, 1988.

Gilbert, Arlan K. *Historic Hillsdale College: Pioneer in Higher Education, 1844–1900*. Hillsdale, Mich.: Hillsdale College Press, 1991.

Gittleman, Sol. *An Entrepreneurial University: The Transformation of Tufts, 1976–2002*. Medford, Mass.: Tufts University Press, 2004.

Gray, Ralph D. *Iupui—the Making of an Urban University*. Bloomington: Indiana University Press, 2003.

Gross, M. G. *Dancing on the Table: A History of Lake Erie College*. Burnville, N.C.: Celo Valley Books, 1993.

Hamilton, Raphael N. *The Story of Marquette University: An Object Lesson in the Development of Catholic Higher Education*. Milwaukee: Marquette University Press, 1953.

Harner, Phillip. B. *Heidelberg College: In Service and Faith, 1950–2000*. Tiffin, Ohio: Heidelberg College, 2000.

Indiana University. *Indiana University, 1820–1920; Centennial Memorial Volume*. Bloomington: Indiana University, 1921.

Jass, Stephanie J. *No Victory Without Work: A Pictorial History of Adrian College*. Virginia Beach, Virginia: Donning Company Publishers, 2009.

Kennedy, Sarah Lehr. *H. R. Lehr and His School: A Story of the Private Normal Schools*. Ada, Ohio: The Ada Herald, 1938.

Kern, Richard. *Findlay College: The First Hundred Years*. Nappanee, Ind.: Evangel Press, 1984.

Klahr, Herman Albert. *Sermons and Addresses of Charles Miller*. Fostoria, Ohio: Gray Printing Company, 1967.

Knepper, George W. *New Lamps for Old: One Hundred Years of Urban Higher Education at the University of Akron. A Centennial Publica-tion*. Akron, Ohio: University of Akron, 1970.

MacNaughton, A. Douglas. *A History of Adrian College*. Adrian, Mich.: Adrian College, 1994.

May, Henry Farnham. *Three Faces of Berkeley: Competing Ideologies in the Wheeler Era, 1899–1919, Chapters in the History of the University of California; No. 1*. Berkeley: Center for Studies in Higher Education and Institute of Governmental Studies, University of California, Berkeley, 1993.

Mc Ginnis, Frederick. A. *A History and an Interpretation of Wilberforce University*. Wilberforce, Ohio: Brown Publishing, 1941

McGrane, Reginald Charles. *The University of Cincinnati: A Success Story in Urban Higher Education*. New York: Harper & Row, 1963.

Rudolph, Frederick. *Mark Hopkins and the Log: Williams College, 1836–1872*. New Haven, Conn.: Yale University Press, 1956.

Peters, John Abram. *Baccalaureate and Other Addresses*. Delaware, Ohio: The Gazette, 1908.

Rudy, Solomon Willis. *The College of the City of New York: A History, 1847–1947*. New York: City College Press, 1949.

Strietelmeier, John H. *Valparaiso's First Century: A Centennial History of Valparaiso University*. Valparaiso, Ind.: Valparaiso University, 1959.

Sweet, William Warren. *Indiana Asbury-DePauw University, 1837–1937; a Hundred Years of Higher Education in the Middle West*. New York: The Abbingdon Press, 1937.

Umble, John Sylvanus. *Goshen College, 1894–1954: A Venture in Christian Higher Education*. Goshen, Ind.: Goshen College, 1955.

Waite, Frederick C. *Western Reserve University, the Hudson Era: A History of Western Reserve College and Academy at Hudson, Ohio, from 1826 to 1882*. Cleveland: Western Reserve University Press, 1943.

Wagner, Paul Alexander. *Rollins College and Dr. Hamilton Holt: Pioneering Higher Education in Florida, Newcomen Address, 1951*. New York: Newcomen Society in North America, 1951.

Watson, Kent, and Peter S. Van Houten. *The University in the 1870s, Chapters in the History of the University of California, No. 6*. Berkeley: Center for Studies in Higher Education and Institute of Governmental Studies, University of California, Berkeley, 1996.

Williams, E. I. F. *Heidelberg: A Democratic, Christian College, 1850–1950*. Menasha, Wisc.: Barta Publishing Company, 1952

Williard, George W. *The History of Heidelberg College, Including Baccalaureate Addresses and Sermons*. Cincinnati: Elm Street Press, 1897.

Williard, George W. *The Life, Character and Work of Henry Leonard: "The Fisherman."* Dayton, Ohio: Reformed Publishing Company, 1890.

Books on State Histories of Higher Education

Allen, William Francis, and David Ellsworth Spencer. *Higher Education in Wisconsin*. Washington, D.C.: Government Printing Office, 1889.

Blackmar, Frank W. *Higher Education in Kansas*. Washington, D.C.: Government Printing Office, 1900.

Bush, George Gary. *History of Higher Education in Florida*. Washington, D.C.: Government Printing Office, 1891.

Bush, George Gary. *History of Higher Education in Massachusetts*. Washington, D.C.: Government Printing Office, 1891.

Dunbar, Willis Frederick. *The Influence of the Protestant Denominations in Higher Education in Michigan, 1817–1900*. Ann Arbor, Mich., 1940.

Dyer, Thomas G. *Higher Education in Georgia: An Historiographical Perspective*. Athens: Institute of Higher Education, University of Georgia, 1976.

Hall, Edward W. *History of Higher Education in Maine*. Washington, D.C.: Government Printing Office, 1903.

Haskins, Charles Homer, and William Isaac Hull. *A History of Higher Education in Pennsylvania, Contributions to American Educational History; No. 33*. Washington, D.C.: Government Printing Office, 1902.

Hoover, Herbert T. *From Idea to Institution: Higher Education in South Dakota*. Vermillion: University of South Dakota Press, 1989.

Le Rossignol, James Edward. *History of Higher Education in Colorado, Contributions to American Educational History. No. 34*. Edited by Herbert B. Adams. Washington, D.C.: Government Printing Office, 1903.

Lewis, Alvin Fayette. *History of Higher Education in Kentucky*. Washington, D.C.: Government Printing Office, 1899.

McLaughlin, Andrew C. *History of Higher Education in Michigan*. Washington, D.C.: Government Printing Office, 1891.

Meriwether, Colyer, and Edward McCrady. *History of Higher Education in South Carolina, with a Sketch of the Free School System*. Washington, D.C.: Government Printing Office, 1889.

Merriam, Lucius Salisbury. *Higher Education in Tennessee*. Washington, D.C.: Government Printing Office 1893.

Parker, Leonard F. *Higher Education in Iowa*. Washington, D.C.: Government Printing Office, 1893.

Sack, Saul. *History of Higher Education in Pennsylvania*. Harrisburg: Pennsylvania Historical and Museum Commission, Commonwealth of Pennsylvania, 1963.

Sherwood, Sidney. *The University of the State of New York: History of Higher Education in the State of New York*. Washington, D.C.: Government Printing Office, 1900.

Snow, Marshall S. *Higher Education in Missouri*. Washington, D.C.: Government Printing Office, 1898.

Tolman, William Howe. *History of Higher Education in Rhode Island*. Washington, D.C.: Government Printing Office, 1894.

Woodburn, James Albert. *Higher Education in Indiana*. Washington, D.C.: Government Printing Office, 1891.

Books on Commercial and Business Education in the United States

Bennett, James A. *The American System of Practical Bookkeeping*. New York: Collins and Hannay, 1826.

Bickham, George. *The Universal Library of Trade and Commerce, or, a General Magazine for Gentlemen. And All Who Are Any Ways Concerned in Business or the Education of Youth. As Well as for Young Clerks, Apprentices &C., &C.* London: Printed for J. Robinson, 1747. 7 pts. in 1 v., [94] leaves of plates.

Bossard, James Herbert Siward, J. Frederic Dewhurst, and Wharton School. *University Education for Business; a Study of Existing Needs and Practices*. Philadelphia: University of Pennsylvania Press, 1931.

Bryant, J. C. *Bryant's Book-Keeping. A Treatise on the Science of Accounts, in Two Parts, Elementary and Practical. Containing a Thorough Explanation of the Principles and Practice of Double Entry Book-Keeping, Adapted to the Use of Universities, Business Colleges, Academies, Public Schools and Self-Instruction*. Buffalo, N.Y., 1869.

Cocker, Edward. *The Guide to Pen-Man-Ship a Copy Book Containing Sundry Examples of Secretary, Text, Roman, Italian, Court and Chancery Hands: With Extraordinary Rules and Directions for Making, Holding & Managing the Pen, and for the Exact and Speedie Writing of Every Hand*. London: Sold by R. Snow and by W. Rumbold, 1664. [1], 12, [25] p.

Dilworth, Thomas. *The Schoolmaster's Assistant: Being a Compendium of Arithmetic, both Practical and Theoretical*. London: Henry Kent, 1768.

Earnest, W. W., and Harry Marc Rowe. *English Correspondence: For Use in Academies, Normal Schools, Business Colleges, Public Schools, Etc.* Baltimore: Sadler-Rowe Company, 1896.

Eaton, A. H. *Eaton & Burnett's Course of Business Training in Commercial Law: A Treatise on Special Topics of Commercial Law Adapted to the Use of Business Colleges, Universities, Academies, and Self-Instruction, with Various Forms of Commercial Instruments*. Baltimore: Eaton & Burnett, 1881. xi, 183 p.

Engwall, Lars. *Mercury Meets Minerva: Business Studies and Higher Education: The Swedish Case*. New York: Pergamon Press, 1992.

Foster, Benjamin Franklin. *The Clerk's Guide; or, Commercial Instructor Comprising the Principles of Trade, Commerce, and Banking: With Merchants' Accounts, Inland and Foreign Bills, Par of Exchange, Equation of Payments, &C.* Boston: Perkins & Marvin, 1840.

Fisher, George. *The American Instructor; or, Young Man's Best Companion*. Philadelphia: Fisher, 1748.

Glasgow Commercial College. *Constitution of the Glasgow Commercial College*. Scotland, 1846.

Graham, Jessie. *The Evolution of Business Education in the United States and Its Implications for Business Teacher Education*. Los Angeles: University of Southern California Press, 1933.

Hanaford, L. B., and J. W. Payson. *Book-Keeping, by Single and Double Entry: For Schools and Academies: Adapted to Payson, Dunton, and Scribner's Combined System of Penmanship*. Boston: Crosby Nichols and Company, 1858.

Haynes, Benjamin R., and Jessie Graham. *Problems in Business Education*. Los Angeles: University of Southern California Press, 1933.

Haynes, Benjamin R., and Clyde W. Humphrey. *Research Applied to Business Education*. New York: The Gregg Publishing Company, 1939.

Haynes, Benjamin R., and Harry P. Jackson. *A History of Business Education in the United States*. New York: Southwestern Publishing Company, 1935.

Herrick, Virgil E. *Comparison of Practice in Handwriting Advocated by Nineteen Commercial Systems of Handwriting Instruction*. Committee on Research in Basic Skills. Madison: University of Wisconsin, 1960.

Johns Hopkins University, Peabody Institute Library, and P. William Filby. *Calligraphy & Handwriting in America, 1710–1962*. Caledonia, N.Y.: Italimuse, 1963.

Knight, C. L., G. J. Previts, and T. A. Ratcliffe. *A Reference Chronology of Events Significant to the Development of Accountancy in the United States*. Tuscaloosa: The Academy of Accounting, University of Alabama, 1976.

Lewis, James Henry. *The Best Method of Pen-Making Illustrated by Practical Observations on the Art of Writing, to Which Are Added, Directions for Holding the Pen Properly, and Many Other Secrets Worth Knowing, to Those Who Wish to Write Well*. Manchester: Printed for the author, 1825. 32 p., [6] leaves of plates.

Lyon, Leverett S. *A Survey of Commercial Education in the Public High Schools of the United States*. Chicago: The University of Chicago, 1919.

Mair, John. *Bookeeping Methodized: A Methodical Treatise on Merchant Accounts According to the Italian Form.* Edinburgh: W. Sands, A Murray, and J. Cockran, 1737.

MacDonnell, J. M., and W. C. Clark. *The Faculty of Arts and Business Training*. Kingston, Ont.: Jackson Press, 1923.

Marshall, Leon Carroll. *The Collegiate School of Business: Its Status at the Close of the First Quarter of the Twentieth Century*. Chicago: University of Chicago Press, 1928.

Marvin, Cloyd H. *Commercial Education in Secondary Schools*. New York: Henry Holt and Company, 1922.

Miller, Jay W. *The Independent Business School in American Education*. New York: McGraw-Hill, 1964.

Mills, Gail A., and American Council on Education. Financial advisory service. [from old catalog]. *Accounting Manual for Colleges.* Princeton, N.J.: Princeton University Press, 1937.

Mitchell, William. *A New and Complete System of Bookkeeping.* Philadelphia: Bioren and Madan, 1796.

Nash, Ray. *American Penmanship, 1800–1850: A History of Writing and a Bibliography of Copybooks from Jenkins to Spencer*. Worcester, Mass.: American Antiquarian Society, 1969.

Rand, Benjamin H. *Rand's Introduction to Penmanship: New Series, in Eight Numbers*. Philadelphia: The author, 1849.

Rice, Thomas A. *Rice's Practical Book-Keeping, Embracing the Theory and Practice of Accounts, Adapted to the Use of Schools, Academies, Universities and Business Colleges*. 2d ed. St. Louis: The author, 1879.

Richards, William. *The Young Clerk's Assistant; or, a Short and Easy Introduction to Trade and Commerce: Consisting of Receipts, Promissory Notes, Bills of Parcels, and Book-Debts, Draughts on Goldsmiths, the Bank, &C, Bills of Exchange, Inland and Foreign, Letters on Various Subjects, Forms of Bills of Entry, Petitions, Invoices, Accounts of Sales, and Accounts Current: With Occasional Directions and Remarks*. London: Printed by J. Hart and sold by J. Wilcox. T. Harris. and B. Cole, 1742.

Sedlak, Michael W., and Harold F. Williamson. *The Evolution of Management Education: A History of the Northwestern University J. L Kellogg Graduate School of management, 1908–1983*. Chicago: University of Illinois Press, 1983.

Spencer, H. C., and Platt R. Spencer. *Spencerian Key to Practical Penmanship*. New York: Ivison Phinney Blakeman; Griggs; Lippincott, 1866.

Spencer, Platt R. *Spencerian or Semiangular Penmanship: Book 13. For Counting House and Mercantile College Utility, Writing Classes, Proficient Students & Learners Generally Business Forms and Ladies' Styles*. Buffalo, N.Y.: Phinney & Co., 1857.

_____. *Spencerian System of Penmanship, American Educational Series*. New York: Ivison Blakeman Taylor and Co., 1873.

Sweet, James S. *Sweet's Modern Business Arithmetic: A Treatise on Modern and Practical Methods of Arithmetical Calculations for the Use of Business and Commercial Colleges, Business Universities, and Commercial Departments in Other Educational Institutions*. San Francisco: Hicks-Judd Company, 1908.

Swiggett, Glen Levin. *College Entrance Credits in Commercial Subjects*. Washington, D.C.: Government Printing Office, 1923.

_____. *Statistics Relating to Business Education in Colleges and Universities, 1921–22*. Washington, D.C.: Government Printing Office, 1923.

Thornton, Richard H. *Principles of Commercial Law a Treatise for the Use of Students in Business Colleges, and Others*. Portland, Oreg.: A.P. Armstrong, 1888.

Thornton, Tamara Plakins. *Handwriting in America: A Cultural History*. New Haven Conn.: Yale University Press, 1996.

Townsend, Calvin. *A Compendium of Commercial Law, Analytically and Topically Arranged, with Copious Citations of Legal Authorities, for the Use of Business Colleges and Universities, Students of Law, and Members of the Bar*. New York: Ivison, Blakeman, Taylor, & Co., 1871.

Turner, Thomas. *An Epitome of Bookkeeping by Double Entry*. Portland, Me.: Jenks and Shirley, 1804.

United States Bureau of Labor, Carroll Davidson Wright, and Charles Patrick Neill. *Annual Report of the Commissioner of Labor: The First-Twenty Fifth. March 1886–1910*. Washington D.C.: Government Printing Office, 1886.

Veblen, Thorstein. *The Higher Learning in America: A Memorandum on the Conduct of Universities by Business Men*. New York: B. W. Huebsch, 1918.

White, John W. *Ledger and Exercise Books*.

Winjum, James O. *The Role of Accounting in the Economic Development of England: 1500–1750.* Urbana, Ill.: Center for International Education and Research in Accounting, 1978.

Workman, Benjamin. *The American Accountant.* Philadelphia: William Young, 1796.

Books on International Education and Cuba

Howe, Glenford D. *Higher Education in the Caribbean: Past, Present, and Future Directions*. Kingston, Jamaica: University of the West Indies Press, 2000.

Books on the Italian Renaissance and European History

Constantinides, C. N. *Higher Education in Byzantium in the Thirteenth and Early Fourteenth Centuries, 1204–1310, Texts and Studies of the History of Cyprus; 11*. Nicosia: Cyprus Research Centre, 1982.

Cowley, W. H., and Donald T. Williams. *International and Historical Roots of American Higher*

Education. New York: Garland, 1991.

Grendler, Paul F. *The Universities of the Italian Renaissance.* Baltimore: Johns Hopkins University Press, 2002.

King, Margaret L. *The Renaissance in Europe.* Boston: McGraw-Hill Higher Education, 2005.

Pacioli, Luca. *Summa de Arithmetica, Geometria, Proporti-oni, et Portionalita.* Venice: Pagininus, 1494.

Radcliff-Umstead, Douglas. *The University World: A Synoptic View of Higher Education in the Middle Ages and Renaissance.* Pittsburgh: Medieval and Renaissance Studies Committee, University of Pittsburgh, 1973.

Rothblatt, Sheldon, and Bjèorn Wittrock. *The European and American University since 1800: Historical and Sociological Essays.* Cambridge: Cambridge University Press, 1993.

Williard, George W., *Comparative Study of the Dominant Religions of the World.* Reading, Penn.: D. Miller, 1893.

Dissertations, Manuscripts, Pamphlets, Papers and Speeches

Davis, James Michael. "Frontier and Religious Influences on Higher Education, 1796–1860." PhD dissertation, Northern Illinois University, 1975.

Gardner, Frank P. "Institutional Histories: Their Contribution to Understanding the American College and University." EdD dissertation, University of Buffalo, 1976.

Articles

Barnes, Sherman B. "Learning and Piety in Ohio Colleges, 1900–1930." In *The Ohio Historical Quarterly* 69, no. 4 (1960): 214–243.

Barnhart, E. W. "Early Beginnings of Commercial Education." In *Vocational Education Magazine* (October, 1922): 101–103.

Hoover, Thomas Nathaniel. "The Beginnings of Higher Education in the Northwest Territory." In *Ohio History*, 1941.

Klopfenstein, Carl G. "TU: Our Beginnings,"

The Challenge Magazine, (Fall 1988), 17.

Reigner, Charles. "Beginnings of the Commercial Schools." In *Education* 42 (November, 1921).

Reigner, Charles. "Notes for a History of Commercial Education." In *The Rowe Budget XXXI.* October, 1929).

Webster, D. S. "Rudolph's American College and University: A History: An Appraisal a Generation after Publication." In *Review of Higher Education* 13, no. 2 (1990): 398–411.

Research and Technical References

Barzun, Jacques, and Henry F. Graff. *The Modern Researcher.* Rev. ed. New York: Harcourt Press, 1970.

Brundage, Anthony. *Going to the Sources: A Guide to Historical Research and Writing,* 2d ed. Wheeling, Ill.: Harlan Davidson, 1997.

Conkin, Paul Keith, and Roland N. Stromberg. *The Heritage and Challenge of History.* New York: Dodd Mead, 1971.

Gall, Meredith D., Walter R. Borg, and Joyce P. Gall. *Educational Research: An Introduction,* 6th ed. White Plains, N.Y.: Longman Publishers, 1996.

Gay, L. R. *Educational Research: Competencies for Analysis and Application,* 3d ed. Columbus, Ohio: Merrill Publishing Company, 1987.

Krathwohl, David R. *Methods of Educational and Social Science Research: An Integrated Approach,* 2d ed. New York: Longman, 1998.

Marshall, Catherine, and Gretchen B. Rossman. *Designing Qualitative Research,* 3d ed. Thousand Oaks, Calif.: Sage Publications, 1999.

The Chicago Manual of Style, 15th ed., Chicago: University of Chicago Press, 2003.

The Compact Oxford English Dictionary, 2d ed. Oxford: Oxford Press, 1991.

Waugh, John C. *Edwin Cole Bearss: History's Pied Piper, a Concise Illustrated Biography of the Life and Times of America's Impresario of Public History.* Washington, D.C.: Edwin C. Bearss Tribute Fund; History America TOURS, 2003.

Index